WUBAS

De'Sean Stacy

For information about ordering books,
or to learn more about the author, please visit:
INSTAGRAM: @deseanstacy
FACEBOOK: De'Sean Stacy

Book design by Michael Quanci
Cover design by DeNiro Elliot
Cover illustration by Diana Lipnick-Feld
Interior photo by Brittany Compton
Printed by IngramSpark

ISBN: 978-1-7365603-0-3

To Aaliyah

CONTENTS

CHAPTER 1

1   The Butterfly Effect

CHAPTER 2

3   A Message for the Mess Age

CHAPTER 3

5   Luminous Being

CHAPTER 4

9   Self-Love

CHAPTER 5

15   The Straw That Broke the Kangaroo's Back!

CHAPTER 6

31   Don't Look Up, Look In

CHAPTER 7

41   T.E.A. is Life

CHAPTER 8

47   Becoming Supernatural

CHAPTER 9

53   A Lithe Body

CHAPTER 10

57   Bet on Yourself

CHAPTER 11

63   Seeing Things Differently

CHAPTER 12

73   WUBAS

CHAPTER 1

THE BUTTERFLY EFFECT

All flowers need mud to blossom.
—Someone Special

As a kid I had a fascination with finding and catching insects. Butterflies in particular. Every time one would fly around it would immediately hold my attention. It would fly around and around from the front yard to the back and back to the front before finally landing on a blade of grass or leaf from a flower petal in my grandma's rose garden. Once it landed, I would crunch down and creep slowly like a cat. Each step was precise, certain not to make a sound. Once I got in arm's reach, I would completely kneel and get really low to the ground—eye level with the butterfly. Then I would slowly reach towards the tip of the wings and quickly snag it. After the catch I would dart inside the house straight to the laundry room near the back porch to find a jar. Grandma always had jars in the laundry room on the top shelf. I would toss the butterfly inside the jar, quickly twist the lid tightly and watch it flutter. After a few minutes I would feel bad and felt that I should free it. So that's what I would do—catch and release. Immediately after I freed it, I wanted to catch it again. I guess it was the chase that got me going.

I remember one time I was in my grandmother's backyard climbing her orange tree. I noticed something hanging from a thin branch. I got closer and realized it was a cocoon; I stood there awestruck and watched it sway in the subtle wind. I really wanted to touch it, but I resisted. Even then I knew that it was a special process that deserved veneration. I began to wonder about the whole process from the caterpillar to the butterfly. I wondered if the butterfly remembered it was once a caterpillar and did the caterpillar know it was going to eventually flower into a butterfly. I still don't know for certain, but I would like to believe on some level there is a remembrance or knowing. Kind of in the same way we humans innately have an inner knowing that our purpose is bigger than just surviving. At our core, there is a longing to grow beyond the caterpillar phase and free our most exquisite inner selves. The longing never ceases until the call is answered. Unfortunately, for most of us, we've made a home in our cramped transitory cocoon. Though it's uncomfortable, we tend to stay there because it's safe, but life will continue to pound away at our shells irrespectively, demanding we answer, ending in either annihilation or freedom, but nothing in between. Though the caterpillar and butterfly are one and the same. The way it perceives the world changes in the spirit of evolution.

In this book you will read about some of the life experiences that have triggered evolution in me. Some experiences hit me pretty hard, and others were just moments of clarity. I've written about those experiences and how they've shaped me into the person I am today. Along with me sharing these experiences I hope to remind the reader that the hurdles and obstacles of life are not roadblocks. Instead, they're steppingstones to elevate you to your highest self.

CHAPTER 2

A MESSAGE FOR THE MESS AGE

Nothing ever exists entirely alone;
Everything is in relation to everything else.
—Buddha

There is a portal that binds and bridges every soul on the planet. At birth the portal is completely open, but as we age it narrows and the connection wanes, disconnecting us from one another and the divinity within. This disconnectedness has always been disastrous for man. For it, man has gradually become a dying breed—by his own hand. Without the voice of the divine to guide us we lose our ability to discern and navigate through life. We begin to categorize, generalize, and calculate everything. All in the name of fear. Fear of getting hurt. Fear of the unknown. Fear of coming out on the losing side of things. But in life there is no losing or winning sides—only growth towards the ultimate.

Over time we have lost sight of this and as a result we've suffered. We've become so entangled in this distorted perception of reality that it's the new normal. Self-deception has deeply melded within our makeup and caused the quality of man to diminish at an alarming rate right before our eyes. We must be proactive about this matter by taking a long look in the mirror. We have to remember who we really are. It starts with an unwavering devotion of the most selfless act in the world—self-love. Through self-love we can expand our consciousness, paradoxically giving back to the world and each other. Taking care of yourself and giving yourself the adequate amount of time and attention, you need to recognize the divine within is not only imperative but it's the sole purpose of life. It's the only way back to love and unity on earth. We're all counting on one another. Within the earth, everything is connected and interdependent on the health and vitality of its constituents. Can you imagine that seven billion some odd people are all depending on the well-being of each other like the cells in a body. Think about it. If one tiny thing goes awry within yourself, no matter if it's physical, mental, or emotional the whole being responds and adjusts. It compensates and eliminates in attempt to heal the afflicted area until it is repaired. Even if the fix is a destructive painful process. Earth, like the self is always thinking about the bigger picture. The earth will rid itself of anything that is not harmonious within it.

To live in your richest skin requires a certain level of discipline and temperance. For most of us, words like discipline and temperance ring the unpleasant monotonous bell of boredom, lack of freedom, and an unvarying colorless life. On the contrary, consistent acts of discipline are the only way to free ourselves and live a life full of zest and joy. Discipline is the way to elation and the highest quality of life. Without it, we move further away from the divine and closer to the beast. Without it, we lose our human connection and compassion for our fellow brothers and sisters. Without it, there is no hope for the children, and without it, we will certainly continue to self-destruct and destroy our wonderful planet as we know it. The selfless practice of self-love through discipline is our only chance at salvation.

CHAPTER 3

LUMINOUS BEING

The highest spiritual state cannot be described,
explained or understood; it can only be experienced.
—Swami S. Saraswati

A t an early age I knew that to be great at anything you had to dedicate a substantial amount of time to practice, and it needed to be daily. One of my favorite self-help books, The Slight Edge, by Jeff Olsen, delves into the theory that small daily habits produce major results. Growing up I played basketball endlessly and watched a lot of NBA games. I studied the players' moves, their jump-shots and even what they said and how they said it on post-game interviews. Allen Iverson and Kobe Bryant were my two favorites. They were trailblazers of the league, doing moves no one had ever seen before. They were flashy and had the coolest shoes. On May 7, 2002, Allen Iverson sat at a podium as he was asked about skipping practice. His response shocked me. He seemed annoyed that the reporter had the audacity to ask him that question. Like he was above it all. Or maybe he felt that he'd done so much for the Philadelphia 76ers organization that missing one or a few practices (I'm not sure how many he missed) wasn't a big deal. I just remember sitting there feeling let down and confused. Here's an NBA superstar with all the talent in the world. I looked up to him, wanted to be like him and play like him. Only to find out that he skips practice. His reasons for skipping may have been justified, but this young kid heard only that he didn't really care for practice. Which made me feel like maybe he didn't want to be the best. I continued to watch him because he was an exciting player, but I never looked up to him again as a player to emulate. I gravitated to watching more Laker games and started studying Kobe Bryant. Kobe possessed a character trait that he became notorious for around the league. His discipline to work on his craft and sweat the small details was said to be second to none. I heard many stories of him working out hours before anyone else got to the gym and hours after they left. I became mesmerized by Kobe's unwavering determination and commitment to be the best. I didn't even want to play like him, mostly because he was much taller and we played different positions. I just wanted his dedication and fearlessness. He was a master at sacrificing instant gratification for something greater. Through his discipline and commitment to be the best basketball player he could be, he taught me self-love.

EUPHORIA

To live in your truest form, you must commit yourself to a practice of self-love. When that practice becomes habitual the most beautiful things commence. Love pervades you and begins to exude out of your very being. Patience, kindness, and compassion develop and become more of a propensity. You forgive as opposed to resenting, and you no longer carry the burden of hate towards anyone or anything. Self-love produces unconditional love for all beings. You no longer have time to hate because you become love. Love is literally the answer to all problems, but it begins with self.

Once you evolve into your higher self through the rituals of self-love you literally become brighter and you start to glow. Your skin heals and you stifle the aging process. Your vision sharpens, colors pop, and the world becomes more vibrant. A sense of youthfulness pervades your entire being. This restoration of energy produces buoyancy in your step and ignites a spark of joy that can eventually turn into a flame of pure euphoria. Being in a state of euphoria is truly our natural disposition. As we've aged, we have slowly allowed the rainy seasons of life to diminish our euphoric flames until we become cold, dark, and dull. Our euphoric flames are like our torches of guiding light in a dark cave. The more we maintain a state of euphoria, the brighter and bigger the flame, and the better we can navigate the world and live in our truest expression. In plain, the happier you are the freer you will become and vice versa.

CHAPTER 4

SELF-LOVE

Control the senses, free the spirit.
—Ancient Kemetic Proverb

The proper maintenance of yourself must start from the inside out, or the outside in, depending on where you're standing. The first step is to revive the integrity and chemistry of the being in its entirety. Extirpating all foods, drinks and substances that are not congruent with the fundamental nature of the being. It will behoove one to look into a cleanse or fast that's suitable to jumpstart this process. The old saying, "You are what you eat," is taken lightly by most, but the truth is, if people knew the severity of it, most, if not all would turn to some variation of vegetarianism. I'm convinced that vegetarianism is the impending future for all.

Once you clean out your gut by eating from the plate of G-d, your entire being begins a healing process. The cloudy specs from your lenses start to clear. Literally and figuratively your vision improves. All the senses regenerate and you start to remember how you're supposed to feel and who you really are. You become your natural self again; hence eating natural foods. It's easier for you to make wiser decisions and you're generally in a better mood. The mind, body and spirit are at peace and your self-esteem and self-respect soar. When you take care of yourself via healthy eating, fasting, yoga, exercising, cleanliness, meditating, praying, reading, creating, learning and taking time for yourself to just relax or reflect and be in nature, you begin to evolve into your higher-self. All this may seem very time- consuming, tedious, and boring. I'll be honest with you, yes, it is, especially in the beginning. But mainly it's the shift in perspective and priority that's has caused us to view these natural customs as additional tasks to complete on our to-do list. In a way, they've turned into chores. Entertainment, social media, excessive chilling, and partying has taken over as top rank in our lives. We've become so materialistic and attached to what's on the surface that we've forgotten that it's what's on the inside that makes us us. It's the sweetness on the inside of the fruit that makes it tasty.

We spend so much of our precious time online or in stores shopping for expensive garments to cover our shameful bodies. Then we fill our bodies with processed fast foods because it's quick, convenient and tastes so good. Since when has sickness been convenient? Then we rush back to work to work more so we can make more money to accumulate more things. We sacrifice our health and mental well-being to try and keep up with the Joneses. I have some cousins who are the Joneses. Trust me, there is no way to keep up with them—I've tried.

Initially it's tough to change for the better. It's going to take every-thing you've got. You'll have to shed so many old habits and adopt new ones. You'll need to unlearn and relearn everything you thought you knew. This will take a significant amount of conscious effort, courage, relentless practice, miles and miles of patience and the will of a god to persevere. At some point you'll feel as if you're losing your mind and you'll begin to question everything. This is good, it means you're on the right path. Internal dialogue will be a moment to moment battle and will get tougher as you continue to press on. You'll feel isolated and sometimes very lonely. Don't worry about that, keep going, it'll change.

Understand, so much of it is rooted in the chemistry of you. Your eating habits are key, but more than anything, a simple shift in what's important will do the trick. Now I know what you are thinking, "This self-love thing sounds really unattractive and next to impossible." But wait! Real quick, before you get all discouraged and overwhelmed. Here's what happens whenever you can persevere through practice and stay patient with the process long enough to obtain the desired result. You gain much more than just that desired goal.

This is what actually happens:
Increase in will power
More patience
The ability to persevere in all areas of life
Increased focus
The cultivation of this newly formed habit
The discipline to give up an old habit
Self-control
Self-love
Whatever benefits the new habit gives
A strengthened mind
Increased self-esteem
Belief in yourself
Respect and admiration from all
Mastery of your own energy
Freedom

You gain all of this and more every time you shed an old negative habit and adopt a positive new one. Oh yeah, and this isn't even the best part. It gets considerably easier overtime; but you have to stick with it until it becomes habitual. From my experience, it was never the end goal that yielded the greatest reward. Rather, it was the act of committing myself for a greater purpose that was most gratifying.

FASTING

Recently, fasting has been reintroduced to the health and fitness world as a great way to keep the waistline slim. Duh. Eat less and you'll lose weight is a simple concept, but for some reason it's become a real eureka moment as of late. Fasting is an ancient tradition practiced across the globe for many different reasons. Still, there are plenty who don't fast. Especially in America, for Americans love to eat. But let us not go in the direction of the obvious. Aside from the long list of the anatomical and biological benefits of fasting, it's one hell of a reminder of who's boss. To abstain from eating at the point of hunger is not a punishment, rather, it's the acknowledgment of G-d. This is why I intermittent fast every day along with a handful of full-day fasts throughout the year.

Most days my stomach begs for food around 9:00 a.m. and again on the brink of noon. Invariably, I turn a cold shoulder to it like an unwanted stepchild. This may seem harsh, but I believe it's good to consciously put yourself through something uncomfortable at least once a day and even throughout the day. This breeds higher levels of consciousness, self-control, and just an overall badass individual. To eat when you're hungry requires no consciousness. Your stomach growls, "Eat," and you do it. What's more, your taste palate then tells you what to eat. Talk about conditioning. Pay attention. It's fine to enjoy your foods, but who's really in charge here? Just food for thought.

Most of us are under the impression that we're freely making choices for ourselves. Well, if this were true, then why isn't everyone living the life of their dreams? Why are so many behind the eight ball? Why are so many sick and unhappy? Simply because there is a shortage of conscious minds. Studies show that roughly over 95% of daily decisions are made from the subconscious mind. Meaning that 95% of your daily decisions are not consciously made by you. Essentially, someone else is living your life, and you're simply going through the motions. If you're not making the decisions in your life, then who is? The docile subconscious mind is bombarded with subliminal messages at the hand of symbols, numbers, colors, encoded images, and sounds that are hidden in billboard signs, media, social media, movies, tv shows, commercials, music, restaurants, apparel, and more: basically all things that play in the background of your consciousness. This is happening 24/7 without us ever knowing it. I mean, we know it, but, we don't. How can we start consciously programming our subconscious minds ourselves? Simply by instilling habits that encourage conscious behavior. Bit by bit, day by day, this can change everything. It's the only thing that can change everything.

SERVANT VS. MASTER

Never become a servant or slave to yourself. You were born a master, but it's up to you to remember and act accordingly. If you allow any impulse to guide you too frequently, then gradually it will lead you to imprisonment. This should never happen. In the often and unfortunate case that it does, it will certainly deepen other issues in your life. Simply because it shifts the consciousness from master to servant. You can't afford to let this shift happen. The lack of self-control triggers a helpless victim mindset that lowers your vibration, resulting in an undesirable troublesome life which becomes calamitous for us all. To serve is benevolent, but if a servant mentality develops within the self, certainly a level of malevolence and rancor will follow. All people were created wholly (holy) and fully equipped to exist as masters within themselves, to serve each other in the name of love for the peace and harmony of all. In the absence of mastery, peace cannot exist.

IT'S ABOUT BALANCE

Please understand, fasting is not one-size-fits-all, nor does it need to look the same all the time. There are times I'll cut it short and have a piece of fruit or a Doctor's Order Green Juice from Whole Foods around ten or eleven in the morning. Depending on when and what I ate the night before. In my humble opinion, fasting shouldn't be extreme or too uncomfortable. At least not every day. Otherwise you could binge in the opposite direction when you do finally get a chance to eat. Do what is suitable and sustainable for your lifestyle. But be sure to do it because it will bring another element of consciousness to your life that wasn't there before.

Start doing something at least once a day that you may not enjoy but you know will make you a better you. Eventually, you'll add another thing and another, and before you know it, you will have completely taken control of your life and be heading in a direction that you chose rather than one chosen for you. My hope is for you to become more conscious day by day. A habit of mindful eating is one of the best ways to do so.

CHAPTER 5

THE STRAW THAT BROKE THE KANGAROO'S BACK!

A woman is to be loved, not understood.
—Osho

On March 3, 2018, I got engaged to a beautiful girl from Sydney, Australia, named Brittany. I remember the day we first met. I was at Ralph's grocery store on Pico and Beverly near the produce. I was standing in front of the sushi bar, with my arms folded, undecided on the shrimp tempura or the avocado rolls. A young girl discreetly stood next to me, mimicking my trance-like gaze. Startled by her presence I plucked out my earphones and started a conversation about the quandaries on which sushi to choose for dinner. Brilliantly she suggested, "Why not both?" We smiled and continued a conversation about her visit to the US. Immediately I noticed her Australian accent. Out of the corner of my eye I noticed another girl casually walking in our direction. Thinly built with big dreamy bluish green eyes with long, dark, brown hair tied into a ponytail that draped between her slender shoulder blades. Her narrow face wore a deep scar that stretched from the outer corner of her thick eyebrow down the length of her cheek. She cradled a bag of purple grapes in her left hand and cracked a coy smirk as she continued to approach us.

"Hello, I'm Brittany," she said.

"Sean, nice to meet you," I replied, as I reached out to shake her hand. I noticed the resemblance and realized they were sisters, but I asked anyway. We exchanged contacts and the next night went out for drinks and dancing.

We were pen pals for many years, and whenever Brittany was in L.A. we would connect. Over the years our bond strengthened, in spite of our inability to physically be together. In December of 2017 she flew to L.A. to visit. We enjoyed each other's company to the utmost. We walked and talked for hours during long hikes up to the Hollywood sign and through Runyon Canyon. At night we would go out to dinner and sometimes a movie. I recall one night in particular. We were at her hotel room getting ready to head to my mother's fiftieth birthday dinner. Impatiently waiting, I sat on the corner of the bed checking social media. Of course, Britt was still in the bathroom with the sink running and music blaring out of a small portable speaker. I ran out of patience and hollered, "Britt, are you almost ready? We need to go. We're going to be late!" She didn't reply. The door slowly swung open as it does in horror movies. She walked out wearing a single-strap black dress that hugged her body so tightly it looked like it was painted on. Not a crinkle in sight. And she wore open-toe high heels that accentuated the tone in her calves and flaunted her fresh pedicure. "Wow!" I whispered; my eyes grew big like Homer Simpson's. Then an increase in blood flow.

"You look incredible!"

"I know," she said, casually shrugging her shoulders followed by a flip of her long, dark hair. Her Chanel perfume was intoxicating, flooding my nostrils as she walked past me to the other side of the bed. She took a few selfies as we made our way downstairs to the Uber.

After all the hugs and kisses and taking pictures with every single member of my family and my mother's close female friends, we were finally able to sit and have a drink and chat with one of my favorite persons—my grandpa. She took a special fondness to my grandpa as he did to her. He sat behind his oversized Cadillac margarita with the red spice on the rim and cracked cheeky jokes and flirted with Britt the entire night. "Oh, my goodness, I love your grandpa's youthful energy! Can we take him with us?" she mentioned a few times that night.

We had a blast that night! Everyone went home drunk, happy and tired. It was a joy to watch Britt get along so well with my family. On the ride back to the hotel, we laughed and reminisced about the celebratory night. I kept thinking to myself, "I wish we could be something more."

ONE PEACE

So, in March of 2018, Brittany and I got engaged. Long-time clients who are like my family allowed me to stay in their guest house until I had enough money to move into a place with my new fiancée. After the engagement Britt flew back to Australia before moving her life to the U.S. for good. We were both so excited and eager to be together. Initially, I thought it would be a better idea if I stayed in the guest house alone, considering that it was meant for only one person to stay there comfortably. Also, to save more money for our own place. Britt saw otherwise and insisted we be together and get our lives started immediately. Against my better judgement I caved and allowed it to be. On April 29, she flew back to the States and away from her homeland, hoping to return only for special occasions. By mid-May things between us ended. Little did I know things were just getting started.

One night, slouched on the couch with my eyes glued to the NBA playoffs I heard a loud wail from the bathroom. I darted to the half open door to see what happened. "Babe, are you okay? What's going on?! Britt, what's wrong?" I asked with deep concern. She was squatted on the balls of her feet with one hand gripping the mouth of the sink and the other holding what looked to be a pregnancy test. She continued to wail; her entire body was trembling. After I asked her again what was wrong, she handed me the test, then I carefully reached in the garbage to grab the box surrounded by balled up tissues. "PREGNANT…" The room started to spin. Her unceasing yowl was drowned momentarily by the weight of the moment. After I got my bearings, I knelt to caress her back, then softly kissed her wet cheek. She continued to sob. Tears of joy, fear, and uncertainty puddled the floor.

From mid-May to the beginning of July was the most challenging time I've ever experienced. The toughest part was that we still had to live together after we decided to break up. Trivial arguments ballooned into explosive fights and sucked the life out of whatever love was left. The energy was rigid and unforgiving, as remnants of happy times gummed to the bottom of our combat boots like dog feces. Love's frail skeleton-like body could be found buried in the back of the closet underneath the things that you forget about and never use. The putrid scent of disdain and depression permeated the guest house like a rotted carcass. Conversations were terse and bitter, and all I could think was, "Just hold it together and make sure she gets home in one piece." I was counting the days to her departure like I was ten years old and it was mid-December. Not only was I still responsible for her until she got back to Australia, but now I was responsible for two. This alone was plenty on my plate. It was all new to us and it seemed to happen all at once. Money also became an issue, because she couldn't work in the U.S. until we were married, and she could legally receive her work visa. The pressure to take care of everything fell on me. Money got so tight we had just enough to eat, get gas, and run errands, while I went back to work. We were literally confined to four walls. Sometimes we took short walks around the peaceful neighborhood after we ate dinner. We marveled at the beautiful two-story homes, thinking, "This was going to be us. We were going to be a family." This killed me, and her too I imagined. Meanwhile, we were on the outside looking in, holding on to the shattered pieces of our relationship.

During these arduous times I remember being pushed beyond my limits in every sense. I saw parts of me I'd never seen before, good and bad. I broke down to exhaustion and became sick with a severe case of strep throat. My torso and arms were covered in hives, and my body would itch to no end. My throat closed up, I could barely breathe. Night-time was the worst, as my illness kept me up till the wee hours of the morning, and when I was finally able to fall asleep from exhaustion, I snored so loudly that it would wake me out of my sleep. At the crack of dawn, I was right back to work with no more than a few hours of broken rest.

Britt and I argued most days. The toughest part was we couldn't figure out how to fix it. We desperately wanted things to be right between us. But once you've created a certain pattern in a relationship it's extremely difficult to break it. It's hard to break patterns within yourself. In hindsight, the longing for peace probably added to the stress. I needed help but didn't know who to ask. I was embarrassed. Some nights on the way home from work after crawling in L.A. traffic I would park a few houses up the block, sit in silence, and think about how to ease the relationship. Rarely am I ever lost on what to do in difficult situations. I would sit and watch the rest of the sun fall from the sherbet colored sky. These moments not only provided me peace, but they were restorative as well. In these short tranquil moments, I was reminded to be understanding and patient. Still, I struggled.

THE NIGHT SHE FELL

From the very first night we went dancing, I knew Britt and I had a strong connection. I picked up Britt and her sister Lauren at their hotel in Beverly Hills, and we drove to meet up with my best friend George at his place in Koreatown. After we hung out in a nearby club for a bit, we ended up at a club in downtown Los Angeles. More of our friends arrived and we headed to the patio. After a short while Lauren headed back into the club. The rest of us stayed on the patio. I was attracted to Britt and wanted her to know it. I stared right into her eyes when I spoke to her. Her cheeks turned red and she looked away. I gently took her hand, pulled her close to me, and whispered, "Can I have a kiss?" She blushed even more, and told me no. After she turned me down a few more times she finally gave in. I pulled her to me, and she gave me a soft peck on the lips. She blushed and grinned so hard afterwards. It was the cutest thing.

"You should go inside and dance with my sister, she's lonely," she told me shortly after we kissed.

I didn't know what to make of it, but I went inside anyway. I was with two hot Australian sisters; I would've done anything they told me. "Why is she pushing me onto her sister?" I thought. "Is this her nice way of shutting me down? Was the kiss bad? I wonder if she's into George?" Lauren stood in the middle of the club dancing by herself. I thought that was courageous of her. People from L.A. rarely dance alone. But she wasn't from L.A., so I guess it made sense. I walked towards her, and instantly our bodies connected like magnets. It was like she knew I was coming. Her back pressed against my chest. She looked down her shoulder and watched me from the corner of her eye. I held her curvy hips and pulled them closer to mine trying to follow her rhythm. I could taste her perfume. The lights came on and quickly broke us out of a lustful spell.

The savory scent of cooking hot dogs pulled my nose to the exit. The little Mexican lady's voice grew louder as we got closer to the exit. Her hot dogs wrapped in bacon always smelled amazing, especially coming from the club drunk. But I had never tried one. Even when I was an omnivore that was too much meat for me. I leaned my back against the wall and waited for Britt and George to walk out. Lauren leaned next to me. Outside the club a sidewalk full of drunk and happy people were pacing back and forth with their friends trying to figure out the next move. Where would the night take them?

I was feeling lucky. Before I knew it, Lauren turned and pressed against me and we kissed. I was shocked but happy. I was living the dream. Right after Britt and George walked out along with the rest of our crew. Britt's eyes glanced at my lips then back into my eyes. My lips were smeared with pink lipstick, though I didn't know it.

Back at George's I could sense Britt was upset. She sat deep in a chair with her arms folded, as quiet as a church mouse. I got up from sitting next to Lauren on the couch and walked over to Britt. I gripped each arm of the chair and leaned over her, invading her space, "What's wrong?" I asked.

"You kissed me, then my sister. That's not cool," she responded.

"Now I see," I thought. "She does have an interest in me. So what made her tell me to go dance with her sister?" I didn't understand that part. From then on, my focus was Britt.

"Well, it's getting late. We should be leaving now," Lauren said after she noticed that my attention had shifted back to her sister.

"Are you about to leave?" I asked Britt. She looked me square in the eyes and shook her head no. "You're gonna hang with me?" Yes, she nodded. I was so happy.

"Well I'm catching an Uber," Lauren said in a reprimanding tone.

"Okay, I'll see you at the hotel later," Britt said.

Lauren grew more upset. "I can't believe you're staying here with total strangers!" Britt paid her no mind. This infuriated Lauren even more, but she tried not to wear it. Britt didn't budge. A notification from Uber dinged on Lauren's phone and she stormed out. After I sobered up a bit Britt and I hopped in my Mustang and headed back to my place. We sped down the 10 Freeway at 3:30 a.m. with the music blasting out the widows. We laughed and sang the whole drive home. Comfort came early and easy for us. She trusted me and I saw potential in her.

Britt took off her heels and laid down on the edge of my bed. My hand reached for the small of her back and inched down to her butt. She smiled and laughed, then grabbed my hand and pulled it back up to her back. "No", she said. Her smile gave me mixed signals, so I tried again. "No", she repeated. She didn't let me take it there. I respected her wishes. I turned on the television and walked into the kitchen. We shared a bowl of watermelon and watched a couple of reruns of Martin. Afterward I took her back to her hotel.

We sat in my car in the front of her hotel lobby. Drake's "Shut it Down" played on repeat and we talked until the sun came up. Around 8:00 a.m. Lauren stormed out of the hotel lobby doors with her arms folded. In mid-stride she took a glaring cold look at us and continued walking in the opposite direction. She was very upset that Britt had left her at the end of the night to stay with a total stranger. But Britt didn't care, for love was already in her heart.

Within love, all other emotions exist. Britt's love was fervid and keen. I love in a different way—silent and gentle. These differences in love languages amongst other things eventually ended our relationship.

A PERTURBED BABY

Initially, we kept our breakup between us. We didn't want to alarm our families about something that we hadn't fully grappled. We were embarrassed at how quickly the relationship had crumbled so quickly. So we kept our story under wraps and played nicely at the family get-togethers. One night, my aunt had an intimate birthday dinner in Santa Monica with a few of our family members. After some hearty laughs, shared memories, and satisfied bellies, Britt and I headed out. During the drive home I could sense something was bothering her. I was afraid to ask, and so I turned on my favorite playlist in attempt to ignore and hopefully lighten Britt's glaring unsettled mood.

"Please, G-d, let this girl be okay," I muttered, rolling my eyes as I reached for the volume knob.

"What did you say?!" she blurted.

Quickly twisting the volume knob in the opposite direction, silencing the music. I could only sigh, "Nothing." I knew that something was really wrong. Palpable tension pervaded the car like heat in a sauna. I cracked my window to relieve some of the pressure and de-fog the front window. The night air slithered through the slit of the window, brushing against my stubbled beard, soothing me like a perturbed baby. The faint whistling sound the air makes when it blows through the crevice of the window was comforting. It pulled my attention away from the imminent argument I could smell like a seasoned blood hound. The mere notion of another possible argument gave me anxiety.

"Can you roll up your window? I'm cold," she said.

I acquiesced. The car was quiet, a bit too quiet. The hum of the engine and the tires wheeling over the asphalt grew distinct. I knew it was much too risky for me to spark a conversation, so I kept my eager lips sealed. So much was said without a word from either of us. "Oh boy, this is dangerous," I worried. Too much silence was a recipe for a fight. The dead air spread the tension as nothing was said. The space seemed to grow between us. Her knees were pushed together, pressed against the passenger door with half of her back pointing towards me. Her arms were tightly folded with her hands tucked snuggly underneath her biceps, folded so tightly that her forearms were resting on top of her breasts about six inches away from her chin. Every so often the leather would squeak, from her arms from rubbing so tightly together. She stared out the window as if there was something that greatly grabbed her interest.

Her body language screamed, "Don't you dare talk to me" and "Please ask me what's wrong," all at once. My stomach bunched into knots from the anxiety as my head pulsed like a heartbeat through a stethoscope. My hands grew clammy on the steering wheel, and my chest and underarms began to gradually heat up like a bagel inside a toaster. A few blocks away from home I rolled down the window halfway, re-inviting the spring night air to cool off my perspiring torso. "There is no way we were going to make it through the night without some sort of argument," I thought. So I pulled the car over on a dark and quiet residential street a mile or so from home.

"What's going on Britt?"

"Nothing," she replied.

"Britt, what's wrong," I repeated. I called her Britt instead of Babe whenever I was irritated with her. It was my way of indirectly saying, "You're annoying me." A moment of silence passed.

"At that dinner party I heard you say you were going to the studio with your brother and your cousin."

"Yeah… and?"

"So, what am I supposed to do while you're gone?"

"Britt, it's almost ten thirty. Can't you just go to bed?"

"Yeah, but I don't want to go to bed alone."

"I understand that, but I'm only going to the studio for less than an hour, and then I'll head straight back home."

"No, you say that, but then you'll be there for two or three hours. I know how you are."

This was too much. "You haven't even lived here since I've been going to the studio with my brother. What do you mean, you know how I am?"

"And don't you have work in the morning?"

"Exactly! So I can't be in there long. I just wanna go and see what they're working on then I'm coming right back."

"Then I'll come with you" she said obstinately.

"No, they'll be smoking, plus the music will be way too loud, and I don't want you around that. It's not good for the baby."

"You don't want me to come because there will be girls there. Admit it!"

"Britt, girls don't go to studio sessions with artists that aren't famous and rich. It'll just be me, my brother, and my cousin. Trust me. I'll call or even FaceTime you when I get there to prove it."

"No, I don't believe you."

"I don't know what to tell you, Britt." The car was silent. I thought maybe she'd given in. "Soooo, I'm gonna take you home now. Then I'll be right back."

"No! You're not!" she countered immediately. Small disagreements were never solved civilly; they usually ended only after all hell broke loose. This time was no different. We went back and forth about it for another ten to fifteen minutes.

Frustrated and tired of this frequent nonsense of arguing I threw my patience out the window and jumped in feet first. With a deep inconspicuous inhale, I roared from the pit of my stomach like a lion, "I'M GOING! AND THAT'S IT!" She responded with a ferocious squealing roar of her own. I couldn't make out what she said. It was more or less of a roar in defiance. Docility wasn't her strong suit, and oddly enough a part of me liked that about her. The problem was she didn't know when to tone it down for the possibility of peace.

The energy got so intense I forgot that we were in a quiet wealthy neighborhood in a car that wasn't soundproof. I immediately brought my attention back to the moment and composed myself. It was very possible that we could've already awakened the neighborhood and someone could've called the police, who are always nearby in these fancy neighborhoods. When we got home, Brit went to the bathroom and shut the door. Ideas of me running out the door, never to return, casually crossed my mind.

She opened the door with a worried look on her face and said, "Babe, my panties have blood spots on 'em". We knew this wasn't normal and so we rushed to the emergency room. It was near midnight as we sat in the car in the hospital's parking lot, both of us terrified to go inside to receive unthinkable news. Tension lingered between us, but we clinched each other's hand for dear life. So much conflicted energy pressed between our palms. I hated and loved her all at once.

Anxious and terrified, we approached the emergency room doors. It all felt like a bad dream or a scene out of a movie. The doors slowly slid open with smoke rising from the floor. The untouched pale walls and bright lights were indifferent and cold. After an intense squint to save my eyesight, my blurred vision settled. Upon entering I noticed two other people slumped down, fast asleep, one with his head leaning and his cheek pillowed in hand, and the other with her body completely folded and her head plopped down between her knees. "How long have they been waiting?" I wondered worriedly. The cold, eerie vibe of the lobby brought us closer, and for a moment we forgot about our differences. Our faces were haggard and weary with dried tears hidden in the creases of our forced smiles.

A nurse approached us and took Britt to the back to run her through a few tests. The nurse signaled me to wait in the lobby. I took another glance at the limp, sleeping man and woman I had noticed a few minutes ago. For some reason, they added to the weight of the moment.

Eventually I was able to go check on Brittany to see how she was doing. A doctor came in to see us after the nurse walked out. He had an apathetic vibe about him, like we were an inconvenience and he had somewhere else he needed to be. Quickly, with his arms folded and conviction in his tone, he told us we should terminate the pregnancy and if we didn't there would be a high probability of her miscarrying.

Tears poured from Britt's swollen eyes as I stood there speechless. With her last bit of strength, she struggled through her sob and sniffly nose to ask a few more questions. I can't recall what questions she asked, but I remember getting upset at the doctor's indifferent demeanor. He stood there with his arms tightly folded, a contemptuous stare on his face, and no indication of compassion. It seemed like he was mad at us. I gently held her hand and rubbed her back until she was consoled enough to get on her feet. We felt so many mixed emotions towards each other and our future. But at that moment, all I wanted to do was hold her and be strong for her.

PRESSURE BUST PIPES OR MAKE DIAMONDS

Right when I thought things could not get any worse, the friends whose guest house we were living in asked us to leave because of a family emergency. It seemed as if my life was falling apart, and at this juncture I collapsed inside. If it had been only me staying there it would've been easy to pick up my things and go stay with a friend or relative. But it was me and the soon-to-be mother of my first child. I had to be steadfast and figure out something quick. For the next week or so we lugged around our duffle bags and backpacks filled with clothes, shoes, and toiletries, living like nomads. We slept on the couch at my best friend's place for a day or two. Then we stayed in a hotel room for a few nights. In the midst of living this nomadic lifestyle, we were in and out of random clinics and hospitals checking the health of the pregnancy, still uncertain of everything.

One day we both decided that if we weren't going to be together then the best thing to do was to terminate the pregnancy. "How could we raise this child in two separate continents? What if she was gonna miscarry anyway? What if the child was going to be weak and sickly from Britt being too stressed from excessive arguing and lack of stability?" We'd asked ourselves and each other these questions every day. It wasn't feasible for us or fair to the child.

So we set an appointment at a women's clinic in West Hollywood. The night before the appointment neither of us slept a wink. The sun rose the next morning, and with heavy hearts and battered faces we drove to the clinic. Neither of us said much to the other and neither of us wanted to be there. But it seemed like it was the right thing to do. While she filled out the paperwork, I sat beside her in disbelief.

"How did I end up here?" I pondered. And I didn't mean just the clinic and pregnancy. I meant my life in general. The fighting, the break-up, the pregnancy, and now homeless. It all seemed to happen in the blink of an eye. The nurse told me the procedure would take a few hours. Once they called her in to the operating room, I headed back to the hotel to get some much-needed rest. As I drove down Santa Monica Blvd. my thoughts were racing a mile a minute. I turned on the radio to distract me from the moment and Kanye West's song "Violent Crimes" started playing. I burst into tears uncontrollably. Tears poured from my eyes like a leaky faucet while the thought of killing a part of me stuck in my mind. I thought, "How could we not give this little person a chance at life? What if my parents aborted me? He or she is a part of us and we're killing it." I felt so ashamed and sad.

Before the song was over my phone rang. I quickly wiped my face with the sleeve of my sweater and cleared my throat. "Mm,mm, hello?" It was Brit on the other end bawling her eyes out. I could barely make out a word she was saying, but I knew she hadn't gone through with the process. She calmed herself enough to say she couldn't do it. I whipped my car around in an illegal U-turn and sped back to the clinic.

We wrapped our arms around one another and held on for dear life. I could barely breathe. I felt her heartbeat pound against mine and we cried and cried. We had no money or a place to live, but this was the happiest moment of my life. I was so proud of her.

CHAPTER 6

DON'T LOOK UP, LOOK IN

To stick to a routine of discipline is hard.
To get back into it is even harder.
—De'Sean Stacy

E very time Britt got upset, I feared for our unborn child. Often, in the heat of an argument I kept quiet in hopes that she would eventually simmer down. Sometimes it worked and other times it didn't. I guess she thought I was ignoring her or just being indifferent towards her plight. It was never either. At times I was just all fought out. This capricious behavior kept me on eggshells. I was in constant thought about how to keep things civil. I felt the well-being of our child and the peace between us was all up to me. Through all this adversity I began to learn serenity. I had no choice. During this arduous time I developed tremendously. My perspective broadened, and I realized that every battle started and ended within me.

On July 1, 2018, the soon-to-be mother of my child flew back to Sydney, Australia. The next day I sat on my mother's couch depleted, reflecting on the two months Brittany and I had lived together in our attempt to build a shared future. Explosive arguments vividly replayed in my mind. The mere thoughts affected me physically. My shoulders would tense, and my stomach would unsettle. The fact that I was still so wholly distressed by past arguments bothered me. Even more, I didn't want to hold ill feelings towards the mother of my child. I felt that the energy I carried towards her could also affect our child.

The next day I went to a yoga class in an effort to shed this terrible feeling. The yoga instructor shared a poem by Jackson Kiddard:

Anything that annoys you is teaching you patience.

Anyone who abandons you is teaching you to stand on your own two feet.

Anything that angers you is teaching you compassion and forgiveness.

Anything that has power over you is teaching you how to take your power back.

Anything you hate is teaching you unconditional love.

Anything you fear is teaching you courage to overcome your fear.

Anything you can't control is teaching you how to let go.

Poems and quotes like this are plastered across the internet by millions daily. Most of the time they have no real effect on the reader other than an internal appreciation and maybe a repost. For me, this serendipitous encounter spoke loud and clear. It seared itself on my mending spirit. More than anything, this poem reminded me of two things. First, I'm in complete control of my response to all things at all times. And second, adversity is not diametrically opposed to serenity but merely a prerequisite to personal development and inner peace. Committing myself to this idea put me back in the driver's seat. Once I came to this understanding and accepted it, I began to act accordingly.

Growing up I was raised by my mother and grandmother. My

grandmother was an avid Christian who kept me in church and taught me how to pray. Every night before bed she would read me a story out of this children's version of the Bible full of illustrations. I looked forward to it every night. If it wasn't too late, she would go into her closet and grab her two tambourines, keeping one and giving the other one to me. We would sing old church songs and dance, shaking the tambourines and twisting our bodies in joy. To conclude our night, we would drop to our knees at the side of the bed and recite the prayer from Matthew 6:6-13, "Our Father, who art in heaven."

Through my grandmother's habitual teachings of Christianity, I understood that my fate was predetermined, and G-d had already chosen the direction of my life. As I grew into adulthood my understanding of this theory changed. My perspective went from looking up, to looking in. In some paradoxical way, beyond human comprehension there is a possibility that both can be true at the same time. Our destiny is already predetermined, yet we still have control of our destination. Either way, I stopped blaming G-d for my misfortunes and stopped asking Him for a better life. I no longer used G-d as a crutch or an excuse. I started to hold myself accountable for the direction and trajectory of my life. Don't get me wrong; I do believe in a higher power, but I don't believe G-d works for me if I don't work for myself. In every holy book it says, "G-d gave us freedom to choose." And if we have the freedom to choose then that puts us in control. We are made in the Creator's likeness. Therefore, we are the creators of our own lives and everything in it.

I embraced this mindset a few weeks after Britt went back to Australia. Spending a significant amount of time alone reflecting and meditating, I knew I had to rebuild and start all over again. I had a child on the way, a small being who would need me to show him or her the way, to lead by example and not by words alone. I knew I could not remain as I was and become the father I had always wanted to be. Especially as a co-parent with the child across the seas. It would take a new version of me, an improved version. I wanted to be an exemplary role model, not only for my child but for myself and others. My inner voice grew so loud that I had no choice but to oblige and give my absolute best effort no matter what it took.

REPROGRAMMING

I quickly grew weary of sleepless nights on my mother's couch. I knew this arrangement could not last long, and the fact that I hadn't lived with my mom since my early twenties really bothered me. When I had moved out of my mother's place in 2008, I had vowed I would never have to go back and live with her. I wanted to be able to stand on my own two feet. Yet here I was. Sleeping on her couch was not only uncomfortable for my body but for my mind as well. Already on shaky ground, I might have spiraled into a deep depression. Instead, I had to use the situation as motivation to pull myself out of the mud.

One day, sitting on my mother's couch hunched and melancholy, I thought desperately, "How will I get back on my feet, back to my old self?" I didn't have any time to waste. Every day that passed I felt the pressure of my impending child's arrival. I'd been a procrastinator my whole life. I couldn't be this way anymore. I had to lift myself up, rise to the occasion, and evolve into a better version of myself.

"But where do I start?" I kept thinking. Randomly, an image of an old book I read and highly recommended flashed in my sullen mind. The Slight Edge, by Jeff Olson. "I'll reread that! Now is the perfect time for me to delve back into a book about building habits," I thought with vigor and optimism.

Each chapter resonated with me more than the first time I'd read it.

Brick by brick I was piecing myself back together. I made some slight alterations in my daily habits. Reading came first. It was something I already enjoyed doing, but I didn't do it religiously. I spent more time on Facebook and Instagram than I did reading. I wanted to change this, so I started to allow myself only 30 minutes a day on social media. Reading became a priority for me; I started with the habit of reading for at least half an hour every day. Then I cut my thirty minutes of social media in half and gave an extra fifteen minutes to reading. I became an avid reader, devouring a book every two weeks or so. Since then I've learned that whenever I cultivate a positive or negative habit, inevitably another habit of congruence follows.

Through reading I learned more about meditation. I had meditated in the past but like reading it wasn't a habit. Starting with only ten minutes a day, I have now increased it to thirty-five to forty-five minutes a day. Sticking with the teachings from The Slight Edge, I knew that it was more important to meditate every day, even for ten minutes, than to insist on spending an hour at it. Through relentless practice, what was once uncomfortable became comfortable. I found myself looking forward to my rituals of self-love and feeling irksome on the rare occasions I missed. Daily meditation put everything else I did on steroids. I found it's the cheat code to life. Meditation was, and still is, the most important part of my day. It's the first practice of my day and the one I look forward to the most. Through daily reading and meditation, I reprogrammed my mind, my self-image, healing myself in every way imaginable.

A WRITER IS AWAKENED

After a few months of living in my mother's place something great happened. My younger brother wanted to give up his apartment upstairs from my mom, because he had some financial setbacks. She asked if I would like to take over his place while he moved in with her. Without hesitation I agreed. I knew having my own place would give me enough mental space to think with clarity and precision to help pull myself further out of the rut I was emerging from. I had just enough money to pay the back pay of what he owed and to cover the next month's rent, due in two weeks. I asked him to leave his bed and the leaky refrigerator with a freezer that would frost anything that was left inside for more than two days. Though I didn't have enough money to get furniture or a new fridge, I was overjoyed to be in my own space.

It was 5:00 in the morning, and the moon was still up, as bright as the light on my phone as the alarm went off. My unwilling body implored me to stay wrapped in the warmth of my sheet and cozy comforter. After a quick motivational speech, I peeled back the comforter and sheet and scooted to the edge of the bed. Reminders of yesterday's grind lingered in the corners of my bones. Cracks and pops sounded from rusted joints like milk pouring over a bowl of Kellogg's Rice Krispies. My unthawed feet trudged against the unforgiving cold kitchen floor. With one hand outstretched for vision and the other aggressively rubbing the crusted flakes from the corners of my eyes. I remembered I didn't have any dishes, so I turned to the broken fridge for a lukecold bottled water. Still in the dark I walked back over and sat on the edge of the unmade bed. The moon light snuck between the crevice of the blinds giving the impression that it was still yesternight. What a mind fuck. Mentally I wasn't there yet, I still needed time to digest reality.

Week by week I pieced together furniture for my studio apartment. Slowly but surely my modest apartment started to feel like home. I stuck with my reading habit and read every day without fail. After a while I was reading a book a week. Not only was this habit of reading feeding me invaluable information, but I noticed a growth in patience, focus, and memory. I loved the person I was becoming. It felt like I was peeling back the layers and unleashing the person I always saw myself as and who I was meant to be. I was beginning to unveil my truth.

One morning at 3:23 my mind was inundated with a bunch of short affirmations that woke me out of my sleep. I didn't know where they all came from, but the words were as clear as day. After a few moments of battling with myself about whether to get up and write this stuff down or go back to sleep, I finally scurried across the bed and into my desk chair. Click, the desk light was on, and a pen was gripped between my knuckles. Before I knew it, the pen took over and scribbled across the paper like a mad scientist on a chalkboard. I could barely keep up. A quick glance at my phone: 4:15 a.m. The pen was finished, and my eyelids began to fall. A quick swivel in the desk chair, and I was back adrift in the abstruse world of dreamland. That was the moment this book was conceived.

When I look back as I'm finishing the book, I see how I grew as a person and a writer alongside the book. It held me accountable to align my energy and my focus with its teachings. It wouldn't allow me to go any other way. That was a beautiful experience.

At the start of this project I was so pumped to write a book. I thought, "Wow, I'll be an author!" I burst through the gates like a racehorse, full steam ahead. Shortly after, reality hit and I thought to myself, "My guy, you barely wrote a decent book report in high school. What makes you think you can write an entire book?" Doubting thoughts crowded my mind most of the time. The truth is, I never saw myself as a writer or someone who could write a book. Many days I struggled to write. In addition to doubting my writing ability, I had to convince myself to spend hours on something that I wasn't really good at. In the spirit of sacrifice, I missed birthday parties, kickbacks, and night's out on the weekends with the guys. That was tough, but day after day I did it. At different times along the journey, finishing the book didn't seem possible. My inner critic got the best of me and I wondered if I was in over my head. But I kept writing anyway. This persevering attitude helped restore my confidence time and time again. After a while I found I could ignore the incessant whispers of my inner critic, and I started writing just for fun. Then I knew I would finish the book, and I began to feel like a writer.

INTERNAL DIALOGUE

Spending all this alone time was great for me. Aside from getting lonely here and there I had to learn how to quiet and control the perpetual voices in my head that grew louder and louder the more time I spent alone. I was conflicted. I loved to be alone, or at least I thought I did. For the better part of the last eight to ten years of my life I had been in and out of relationships, rooming with different friends and family, always with the nagging thought in the corner of my mind that I really longed for more time alone. Thinking I would have unlimited time to learn, create and grow into the ultimate version of myself. Sometimes I had even secretly resented the woman I was dating at the time because I felt she was stealing my limited time.

Now I had what I'd always wanted—a small place of solitude and peace I could call my own. I no longer had anyone to point to and say, "They are really slowing me down." Once I was all alone, the struggle shifted from not having enough time alone to having too much time alone. The dialogue switched from external to internal, which is just as hard to deal with, if not worse. Intermittent thoughts about hanging with friends and blowing off my responsibilities and commitments grew more attractive the longer I stuck to the script. These were the same commitments I had made to myself when I was up to my earlobes in motivation. It got to a point where I began to question everything; I felt like I was going mad. "Why am I working this hard? How long will I have to work this hard until I become successful? What if I never become successful and I did all this hard work for nothing? Am I fooling myself? Am I just spinning my wheels? Maybe life is fixed, and no one actually has control of their destiny." These thoughts often crossed my mind.

Many nights I sat in my reading chair and contemplated giving up. "Just be normal and do whatever gives you pleasure. Why work like this with no guarantees of a reward at the end? Why sacrifice so much? No one else is doing this." These thoughts repeated in my mind. The nights were the toughest.

Here's what my Monday through Friday looked like: wake up at 5 a.m. meditation from 5:10-5:40, then squeeze in object writing for ten minutes (a daily exercise to become a better writer). Quickly juice celery and make a green tea for the road. Get dressed and be out of the house by 6:15, 6:20 latest. Anything after 6:20 and I was for sure late to my first appointment. And if I was late to my first, subsequently I was late for each one after that. Then after my morning clients were done, I had to work out myself. Couldn't be a hypocrite. Not only did I have to work out, but if I don't kill the workout and give my best each time, then I'm sure I'm fooling myself and wasting time. After the gym, shower get dressed, get lunch and get a quick 10- or 20-minute nap to recharge and have enough energy to finish the second half of my appointments. Wake up, read for 45 minutes or an hour and write right after that, until I have to go back to work to finish my evening clients.

While driving to and from clients I often listened to a Spanish podcast or Spanish music. That was the only time I could give to learning Spanish, which I really wanted to learn. On the ride home I listened to classical or jazz music, or I drove in silence. This was my time to reflect on the day. Every night on the ride home I pondered two things: how to abate my productive but arduous schedule, and how much longer could

I keep this up. Finally, after driving through 35 or 45 minutes of traffic, I arrived home to have just enough time to prep for the next day and go to sleep. Prepping consisted of cutting up fruit and vegetables for lunch, writing my schedule for the next day, making dinner, and taking a shower. Then right on to sleep or I would be late to bed.

The anticipation of doing it all over again the next day was daunting to say the least. "I could barely make it through today," I thought. "Just give in and be a regular dude. Trying this hard for something is crazy. Are you a maniac?!" Justified thoughts of quitting echoed EVERY SINGLE DAY! After some time of winning those internal battles and losing a few, I knew I needed help. But I was too stubborn and embarrassed to ask anyone. Nor could I afford to pay for a professional. These ponderous moments were too heavy for me to lift alone. I have a go-to book full of inspiring quotes from poets, writers, philosophers, and humanitarians. I skim through it whenever I'm at a crossroad or feel like throwing in the towel. I use it like a spiritual guide.

As I mentioned before, so much of internal dialogue is rooted in the chemistry of you. The chemistry of you can go from natural to unnatural, moment to moment, depending on the chemicals ingested via food, air, and the environment. The hardest part of life is that the dialogue never ends. The key is to lead and control the direction of the conversation.

CHAPTER 7

T.E.A. IS LIFE

*When you are evolving to your higher self the road seems lonely. You're simply
shedding energies that no longer match the frequency of your destiny.*
—Someone Beautiful

PEOPLE

Your time, energy, and attention are your most prized possessions and the
real currencies of the world. If these are managed properly, you will begin
to feel like you are the richest person in the world. If they're mismanaged
for too long, you could find yourself in a deep depression, or even worse,
wanting to die. Nowadays, managing your attention may be one of the
hardest things to do. Most of the time you don't notice that something
has grabbed your attention until you realize you've already been grabbed.
During writing sessions I've found myself ping-ponging on which word
to use. I'd open my phone to go to my dictionary app, and before I knew
it, I would be responding to clients' text messages or clicking random
links in the notification center. And what do I always tell myself when this
happens? "I just need to send this one text then it's back to writing." Then
one text turns into two, and before long I forget why I was on the phone
in the first place. Let alone which word I was looking for.

What's scarier is that I don't have a television in my place, and I abhor
social media. This isn't the case for most. Especially for those of us living

in Los Angeles, the mecca of entertainment and distractions. After so many failed attempts to resist the urge I got smart and did the unthinkable. I put the phone on airplane mode and got twice as much work done in half the time and never lost a client because of a delayed response.

Turning your time, attention, and energy to the right things is a major key to your happiness and success. I find that the more time I spend alone investing in myself, the better I become when I'm around others. I'm also eager and excited to be with them. Be mindful of who you share yourself with. In a non-egotistical way, you need to see yourself as an invaluable rarity; and that's because you are. There's only one you, designed in a unique way with special qualities and skills to be cultivated and shared with the world.

Be kind to all, but share yourself with only a few. Invest your energy only in people who also make self-love a part of their daily diet. I promise you these people are going to help you improve without even trying. Just by being themselves, their positive traits will begin to rub off on you and vice versa. There'll be no room for anything else. The energy will be reciprocated, and neither party will feel like the other is leaching off their energy or resources. There's a reliable indicator as to whether you should invest your time and energy in someone: how you feel when spending time with them, and how you feel once you've left them. If you feel like you're not appreciated, if you're drained, exhausted, or agitated, then this is not a person you need to spend your time with. Cut them off immediately! It's imperative to your wellbeing and growth. Your peace is really all you have. And you can't worry about hurting their feelings or trying to make them understand why you had to make this decision. This is not your job. It's not about saving everyone's feelings. It's about protecting and mastering your own energy by any means necessary. Even at the expense of disconnecting with friends or family.

The best way to help this type of person is to not help them at all and leave them be. This forces them to shift their focus on themselves. They can no longer use you as a crutch or a point of blame for their inauspicious circumstances. Once they shift their focus to themselves, they begin this self-screening evaluation process. All their flaws and the areas they need to work on stand out. Then they start to develop a sink-or-swim mentality. Do you see what's happening? They're forced to look deep within themselves to see what they're made of. They come to a realization that they could never reach with you there as their crutch.

With the right person, reciprocal time and energy invested will not be draining in any sense. People who love themselves will have ample space and time to love you. The reciprocation of this uplifting energy will be recognized by both parties. They will understand that time spent together is a wise investment on all levels.

So many people give their attention, time, and energy to the wrong things and people. Some do it because they've found comfort in the dysfunctional, destructive habit or relationship they've cultivated over time. Some are hopeless and can't see a way out. They've become so deeply rooted in the behavioral pattern or relationship that it has become their truth. They can no longer see the trouble with it. They've become stuck.

START READING LIKE YOUR LIFE DEPENDS ON IT, BECAUSE IT DOES

After a full day of work or school most people come home, plop down on the couch and delve right into TV or social media. Instead, you should adopt the habit of daily reading, even if it's only for fifteen or twenty minutes. Just be sure to do it every day, or at least more days than not. I promise you this habit alone will immensely change the trajectory of your life. When you start one habit, eventually another of its nature will follow, resulting in a stock full of positive or negative habits. Daily reading helps reinforce a positive perspective and improves focus and communication skills. It also expands the mind, breeds creativity and ideas, and opens more options for intellectual expression.

Reading exposed my scrawny vocabulary. In every book I read I highlighted the words I didn't understand. Some books felt like they were written in a cryptic language. The whole page was covered in neon yellow sharpie. Not only did this humble me, but the more I read the more I realized how much I didn't know. Afterwards I would go back and write down each highlighted word on a flash card with the definition on the back. The next time I saw the word I either knew what it meant exactly, or I could surmise the meaning from the context. This habit increased my reading speed and comprehension exponentially. Not to mention my confidence as well.

DISTRACTIONS

We live in a time where our attention is under attack 24/7 by the media, social media, notifications, text messages, emails, friends, etc. There is a palpable decline in the attention span of the youth. It has even affected the elders as well. This decline has slowed our productivity and our ability to finish tasks. That directly affects how we measure our self-worth. Our attention is spread too thinly, causing us to lose focus on any one thing for any length of time. This fosters frustration and disappointment.

You cannot know your value or purpose until you have given yourself enough attention and time alone to recognize it within yourself. The hardest thing to deal with is having the feeling of not being able to express yourself in your truest form. Even if you don't realize it. The true self (spirit) requires ample time alone to remember itself then express itself.

When impeded from doing so, all hell could break lose. When you don't actualize your gift (yourself), it begins a rotting process which starts to alter your true nature. This can become extremely uncomfortable and hazardous. You regard yourself with disdain and begin to live through the eyes of your ego instead of your spirit. Moving further and further away from your true self (G-d). The ego strengthens over time due to a lack of confidence. Confidence wanes over time due to a lack of attention given to self. I've learned the value of my attention and the importance of directing it towards what is most important. Like a laser beam, the thinner it spreads the weaker it becomes. Redirect your energy towards yourself and only share it with those who deserve and can multiply it. Your time is money, spend it wisely. Narrow your attention, eliminate distractions, and filter out the mental garbage. A little garbage is okay, but don't overdo it.

To all the students studying hard to get good grades, keep it up. The act of studying alone is invaluable. It strengthens the brain like exercise does for the body. But it isn't enough. More importantly you must find what you love and submerge yourself in that. Then go towards what you fear the most and learn about that. Learn everything you can about everything. Expand your consciousness. This is when learning becomes effortless and fun.

CHAPTER 8

BECOMING SUPERNATURAL

*Changes cannot be accomplished and will not be forthcoming
if the diet has not changed.*
—Dr. Sebi

I t wasn't until I formed the nightly routine of cutting my veggies for
dinner and my fruits for tomorrow's lunch that I experienced the
spiritual connection man has to food. Every night for about thirty
to forty minutes I had a spiritual experience I fell in love with, just by
cleaning and cutting produce. During this nightly routine I perceived the
healing properties of natural foods, and a feeling of gratitude came over
me. I stopped seeing it as boring and time consuming and understood
this was time invested. Every time I went through this process, I reminded
myself to have patience and stay present. My countertop was covered with
splashes of water and colorful fruits and vegetables. The sight of it brought
me joy. I imagined munching on slices of cold, crispy Fuji apples, along
with soft, bright yellow, sweet mangos and crunchy, refreshing cucumbers
(to name a few) the next day to end my fast. Even the sound of the knife
hitting the cutting board was therapeutic. The focus and precision it re-
quired pulled my attention to the moment and gave me peace. The whole
process became an enjoyable experience. Not to mention the angelic voice
of Sade reverberating off the kitchen walls, serenading me while my mind
was free of thought.

On a deeper level, eating from the earth is one of the best ways to connect with G-d. It increases your consciousness, filtering out the junk that dulls and alters the mind. The chemistry of your being is restored, and information pours from the source with directness and clarity. Shifting your diet towards natural foods is not a one-size-fits-all endeavor. I'm not saying that everyone needs to only eat fruits and vegetables. I'm simply saying that you need to eat what's chemically congruent with your body. I am saying that if an increase in energy and a better mood is what you're looking for, then the bulk of your diet needs to be nonanimal, whole plant-based, organic foods from the earth.

Everyone has a unique body that is efficient or deficient in different nutrients. The goal is to find out what you lack and then supply it. On the flipside, a nutrient in excess doesn't get absorbed by the body. Instead, it gets filtered and then converted into waste. So please don't run to the vitamin shop and buy all the same vitamins your best friend is taking or follow these fad diets. The best way is get really in tune with the body by educating yourself. Or go see an Ayurvedic specialist, who can not only tell you what foods are best for you specifically, but also what foods go well together for digestion and when to ingest them. As I've said, each body has different needs. Over time, we've gotten caught up in what tastes good instead of what's good for us. We must treat ourselves as we would treat a small child and encourage ourselves to eat plenty of fruits and veggies, because we know it'll make us healthy and strong.

ERADICATING MEAT, THEN REFINED SUGAR

For so long I resisted the idea of eradicating meat from my diet. A myriad of excuses ran through my mind every time I gave any consideration to becoming vegetarian. The truth is, I was scared. Attached to my favorite drinks, foods, and desserts, I couldn't imagine them erased from my diet. So I turned my nose up at the idea and carried on with my usual eating habits none the wiser.

As I approached my late twenties, my body began to speak an unfamiliar language. Aches and pains wore out their welcome, and acute injuries took twice as long to heal. After meals I felt a slight bulge and discomfort on the right side of my stomach, uncomfortable and at times painful. This trouble was new to me as I hadn't felt it before. Over time it didn't go away. I grew concerned but didn't say anything to anyone because I'm a man, and men do stupid things like that from time to time when it comes to our health.

One night in the wee hours, I was wakened by a stabbing ache in my stomach. I tossed and turned and curled into a ball trying to abate the agonizing pain. I crawled out of bed and made it to the floor. The cramp was so intense I couldn't stand up straight. I staggered to the bathroom groaning in anguish, hunched over with one hand holding my belly and the other pressed against the wall. I sat on the toilet seat completely folded over, chest to thighs, begging G-d to free me from this torturous pain.

"What did I do to deserve this? I'm a good person! Why me G-d, why me! Ugggghhh!" I yowled and hollered and yowl and hollered. "Ugggghhhh! G-d, please help me!" I cried. After ten minutes my whole body was trembling and dripping in sweat. It felt like I was boiling. Pellets of sweat fell from my face to the floor. My thighs were slipping and sliding on the toilet seat. The pain wouldn't let up, and it lasted thirty or forty minutes. That short amount of time felt like a lifetime, and I was in tears. The level of pain I felt that night I wouldn't wish on my worst enemy. I was in hell's hell, to put it mildly. That night shook me up enough to make a change.

A good friend sent me to a holistic-herbal doctor, who put me on a meatless diet consisting of only fruits, veggies, and water or tea for two weeks and gave me some herbs to take. In addition, he instructed me to take two or three tablespoons of extra virgin olive oil every day for two weeks. In a few days, the discomfort I usually noticed in my gut after meals was no longer there. I reckon it disappeared by the second or third day of the meatless purge, but I followed through with the cleanse to its completion, just to be safe. Finally, at thirty-four years of age, I made a decision to cut out meat from my diet Monday through Friday, consuming organic grass-fed palm size portions on weekends only. The partial commitment softened the anticipated shock. After a week or two I noticed a subtle drop in my energy after my meat-eating weekends. By the third or fourth week the cravings for meat vanished, though I still ate it out of habit. My sluggish start into the week became more and more pointless and uncomfortable. In contrast, my cravings for increased energy and focus from the vegetarian weekdays were insatiable.

One day on a routine visit to my favorite restaurant, Simply Wholesome, I stumbled across the last copy of an eye-opening book hidden between the backs and shoulders of other health books, Sugar Blues by William Dufty. After binge reading it in two days I knew this was the next step. Cutting out processed sugar healed my body from the inside out. A recurring rash on my elbow disappeared in three days, along with all my joint pain. My skin grew clearer and I noticed another boost in energy and mental clarity. I felt like my twelve-year-old self. I was happy as a Cheshire Cat, but nothing in my life changed other than a shift in diet. Then I knew there was a direct correlation between happiness and diet. Not only are our levels of happiness contingent on what foods we consume most, but our diet plays a huge role in making sound decisions.

THE PROCESS OF THINGS

On any given night after a long day of work, the last thing I feel like doing is coming home to prepare tonight's dinner and tomorrow's lunch. It's 7:30 at night, maybe a bit after. I'm beaten and worn out; my gym bag slips off my sore shoulder to the floor. I'm right behind it, plopping down on my chaise lounge. "Finally, my day is over," I think to myself with a big sigh of relief. Bits and pieces of the day linger my mind, along with a barrage of tasks that pick at my attention. My stomach grumbles and reminds me I still have to make dinner. "Okay, okay, what's for dinner?" I ask. "I just wanna order something from Postmates," I say to myself while rubbing my achy neck and shoulder. Then I realize that ordering something will take just as long as making my own dinner. "At least if I make my own dinner, I'll feel happier when I'm finished."

And why is that? Why do we always feel happier after we've made the tough choice of cooking at home versus ordering takeout? On a conscious level we think because we're saving money and it's healthier for us. And we're right. But on a deeper level, it's because we did what's harder and stuck to the plan we made earlier that morning or week. We didn't allow fatigue or other excuses to control our decision. We exercised discipline and patience to go through the monotonous process of preparing, cooking, and cleaning up. Even if the meal was easy and a short process. Rarely do we ever plan to order takeout at the beginning of our day, unless it's a treat or we know we'll be out late attending some prior engagement. Otherwise, takeout is usually a last-minute choice that's made from a tired, unwilling mind, unless the fridge is empty. Going out to a nice restaurant is a totally different story we won't get into because it's irrelevant in the matter.

It's not so much the time it takes in preparation than it is the process of going through it all. There is a lack of patience, not a shortage of time. If it were about the time and we didn't want to be up late cooking, most of us still wouldn't order food. We'd just prepare for bed and skip dinner altogether. Or in the worst circumstance, we would go into the fridge or cabinet for a light snack and call it a night. But most of us will say we don't have enough time to cook, and then we order food that takes just as long to get here. We're too tired when we get home from a long day to prepare anything. The mere idea of it exhausts us. We'd rather sit and watch TV or check social media while waiting on some stranger to handle our food and deliver it to us lukewarm.

Trust me I get it. I'm a bachelor who lives alone and can't cook a lick. My lack of cooking skills is one of the reasons my diet consists mostly of raw organic produce, whole grains, and nuts. Still, we must find it in ourselves to eat at home (most of the time) with the highest quality ingredients (all of the time). Though I am vegetarian, my diet is still a work in progress. I'm unsure if there is such a thing as a perfect diet. Just keep refining and learning what foods work best for you and your lifestyle. Your eating behavior should breed a certain level of consciousness; and if it doesn't then you probably need to reevaluate your dietary habits. Understand, the welfare of the world is contingent upon the gut health of mankind.

Opportunities to reinforce discipline and patience run through the day from the moment we open our eyes to the moment we close them. Routine moments like not hitting the snooze button when it's time to wake up, making our beds, breaking the fast with a green juice or a piece of fruit, being diligent during work or focus hours and not checking social media or emails, and flossing and brushing before bed. These all seem insignificant, but if practiced religiously and assuredly a considerable increase in discipline will follow, along with patience. The more times you activate these muscles throughout the day, the stronger they'll become and the more evident in all the areas of your life. Be patient, be disciplined and don't get caught up in the rat race of life, attempting to rush through everything. Life is beautiful when you slow down and submerge yourself in the process. Even cleaning and cutting fruits and vegetables.

CHAPTER 9

A LITHE BODY

Every form of life is continuously refining itself
and moving towards perfection.
—Swami S. Saraswati

SLENDER MAN

Almost every day of the summer of 1997 I walked to Hollywood Park on 120th to play basketball. There was a tall and lanky old man there most of the time, drinking his beer covered in a brown paper bag. One day, after I shot a few shots, he walked over to the courts and asked to shoot the ball. Actually, he sat his beer near the grass and just started shooting with me without ever asking. Most ol' heads from my neighborhood would do that kind of thing. He said, "Youngster, what you know about this game?" as he picked up my ball and cocked it behind his head for a long jump shot. Swish! "Lucky shot," I thought as I caught the ball from the net. I passed it back to him and he shot it again. Splash! Nothing but net again. "Okay, this drunk old man is really getting lucky," I thought as I passed it back for the second time. This time he's in mid-sentence as he slingshots it over his head. Swish! I was sold. "Okay, this old man can shoot."

After his third swish in a row I was impressed but also annoyed that my solo shoot around had turned into me rebounding for some old drunk. So I threw him a bad pass hoping to break his streak. Finally, he missed. "Aw youngster, you gotta make a better pass than that," he said, followed by a loud belch. After chasing down the long rebound, I walked back on to the court. In just that short amount of time my whole perspective of the old man changed. I had become interested in him. He bent down to grab his beer, and that's when I noticed his huge hands. His fingers snaked around the beer bottle like tinsel on a Christmas tree.

"Can you palm the ball?" I asked. He opened his palms to me wide, signaling for me to pass him the ball again. His oversized hand wrapped around the ball as he outstretched his arm like he was Michael Jordan. "How can I get to palm the ball like that?" I asked.

"Stretch," he responded.

"My hands? How do I do that?"

He showed me a few techniques to practice. He said, "Do these every night and after a while you'll be able to palm the ball too."

"What if I stretch my entire body? Will it help me grow taller?"

"Yep," he assured me. Wow, I felt like I had a secret no one knew about. "Not only will you grow taller, but you'll never get injured," he followed.

I was psyched! I wasn't the tallest, most athletic or the most talented out of my friends, so I was always looking for a way to get an edge. From then on, I stretched most nights before bed and at random times throughout the day hoping to grow taller and one day soon be able to palm a basketball. I'm only 6'0" on a good day, but now I can easily palm a basketball, and I can count on one hand how many times I've had a significant noncontact injury from exercise or playing a sport. From this experience I've preached stretching and flexibility to anyone who's asked me how to stay in shape.

BODY IN MIND

As I mentioned earlier, the quality or nature of the mind relies on the integrity of the chemistry of the brain and body. A well-oiled, conditioned, limber body is next. Exercise is scientifically proven to improve the chemistry of our mind, thereupon boosting our sense of well-being. More and more people are exercising for the mental benefits of movement, with the physical benefits secondary. Through my years of playing sports and exercising as a small boy and now well into adulthood, I've accumulated unavoidable acute injuries as all athletes do. At twenty-three years of age I decided to become a fitness professional. I studied religiously about the mind's and the body's response to physical exertion. After years of studying and experience I've come to the conclusion that keeping the body limber is not only the way to drastically decrease the risk of injury and significantly boost one's overall performance, but it's also one of the major keys to the fountain of youth. I would even say that the mobility of the joints and the optimal length of the muscular system is the most important facet in all sports and forms of exercise. Simply put, add yoga or some sort of stretching regimen into your fitness routine.

The benefits of stretching for the body are not only logical but endless. But how does a lithe body help the mind? I thought you'd never ask. The mind and body rely on the peace and ease of the other, or the lack thereof. An inflexible body is not only uncomfortable, but it also quickens the fatigue of the mind significantly. Optimal mobility releases channels of blocked energy trapped in the rusted corners of the body. It eliminates aches, pains, and resistance from the body, so that movement becomes effortless and free. Like when we were kids. It also realigns the body for optimal functioning. When the body is realigned, everything in your life realigns as well. Relieved of these aches and pains, the mind is more present, with more focus, power, and energy to do as you please. Keep the body limber and fluid then the mind becomes happy and serene again. The happier the mind and body, the more energy you'll possess.

CHAPTER 10

BET ON YOURSELF

You miss 100 percent of the shots you don't shoot.
—Wayne Gretzky

For my second birthday my dad bought me a Fisher Price court. He would put the court on one side of our glass living room table and me on the other. He would hand me the squishy, miniature size basketball and in a lively tone yell, "Shoot, Seany, shoot!" Swish! He'd get so excited that a smile would stretch across his face to the other side of the living room. All his teeth would show like a row of dominoes. My mother told me he would get more excited than I did. He would quickly grab the ball and hand it back to me to shoot again. "Again Seany, shoot!" Again, swish, nothing but net! Maybe sometimes it would bank off the backboard but either way it went in and my dad would go nuts! My mom would sit at our modest dinner table, sipping her coffee sweetened with hazelnut creamer and a few teaspoons of sugar. "Stephanie look," my dad would shout to my mom. "He's making all of his shots! Look at 'em!"

My mom would crack a smirk. "I see him Eddie, I see him," she'd utter in a slight perturbed tone. She wouldn't get nearly as excited as my dad would. Then right back to sipping her coffee and organizing her thoughts. My dad brought home the bacon, but my mother kept the house in order. She was a young mother and I was her first child. It was all new to her and she wanted to be a good mother. She usually had plenty on her mind. Too much to sit down and shoot hoops with us.

At five- or six-years young I knew what I wanted to be when I grew up. My mother would ask me, and I would tell her proudly with my chest pumped to the sky, "I'm going to the NBA. And after I'm done playing, I'm gonna be a coach. That way I can stay in the NBA and I won't have to look for another job." I had it all figured out. No one could tell me otherwise. Even then I knew I didn't want a regular nine-to-five job like most people. Little did I know, every other black boy in the city had the same dream as me.

My mother and father split up when I was six. Soon after we moved to my grandmother's. She lived in a house on a quiet residential street where she raised my mom and uncle. Though my grandmother jumped in as fulltime parent, still, she wasn't my father, nor was she adept with the ins and outs of youth sports. I lost the guidance and support I needed to navigate through the elaborate world of youth basketball and sports. My first love was basketball. Basketball every day all the time. I was an average height for a kid but for a basketball player I was considered short. It wasn't until we took team photos that I realized I was usually one of the smaller guys on the team. My undersized frame and average speed forced me to develop solid dribbling skills and later recognize the importance of an outside jump shot. My intense love for the game helped polish my skill without much help from a coach or trainer. Late nights after dinner and homework I would sneak to the backyard and shoot hoops against other imaginary players. I knew if I'd ask, there was a possibility my mom or grandma would tell me, "No, it's too late to go outside. Go take a bath and get ready for bed."

Not playing ball wasn't an option for me. It was a part of me like my arms and legs. It still is. For most of my boyhood, I played on a small, square, wooden backboard held in place by two short, rusted metal rods welded into the roof of the garage, and no rim to shoot at. The basketballs my mother bought me were made of cheap rubber and for some reason always turned lopsided only after a few times of usage.

Where I grew up no one had a trainer. At best, your father was your trainer, and for my friends who were lucky enough to have their dads in their lives, those dads coached them, and they trained hard. Maybe sometimes too hard. Fathers did not take it easy on their sons. Not only did the dads train them hard, they put them on the right teams with the right coaches if they were not the coaches themselves; and they rarely skipped a season. They understood the minutia of youth sports. They also had another huge advantage over the kids like me that didn't have a dad to help train and teach them the game. That was post game talks. Those talks may be the most valuable gift a young player can receive from his dad, trainer, or coach. Although I know all players across the globe hated post game talks as a kid.

I feel their pain as I write about it. Many times I've sat in the back seat with a teammate after an intense basketball game on a Saturday afternoon listening to him get grilled by his father about his lackluster game. In these moments I was happy my dad wasn't there to do the same. After playing your heart out the last thing you wanted to hear was your dad's heavy voice reverberate through the inner walls of his pick-up truck, giving you advice on your lack of shot attempts and continually repeating, "You need to sprint full speed up the court!" Meanwhile you're in the back seat staring out the window with your oversized jersey drooping on your scrawny shoulders and your sweaty back glued to the hot leather seat. Munching on your snacks while intermittently sipping on your Capri Sun given to you by the team mom who never seemed to give you the bag of chips you wanted. Not to mention you already felt like crap because you didn't score any points and you barely received any passes from your teammates.

You having a good game was important to your father. He could not be the father of the sucky son who always caused the team to lose. Especially if you're black! This was and still is a huge no-no in the black community. In retrospect, any player who can attest to this is thanking their fathers tenfold for these embarrassing, uncomfortable moments. If you're lucky, you got a talk from your dad and your coach, if they weren't the same person.

Post-game talks are invaluable. As the player, you have a chance for someone more knowledgeable about the game to break down to you what was really happening in the game. Because what you see happening and what's actually happening in the game are two totally different things. You need your coach's perspective to explain to you what really transpired so the next time you play you can catch it. This quickens your understanding and confidence tremendously. The game is mainly mental, and confidence is everything. CONFIDENCE IS MORE THAN 50%.

As a kid I played for the love of the game, like most kids. The thought of going to the NBA and what preparations I'd need was a thought I could address down the road. Something I could deal with when I got to college. Boy, was I wrong. This is where having a dad or some type of mentor really helps. It wasn't until later that I understood that the superstar players I played against in high school were being groomed since they were ye high. Moreover, it was the constant instilling of confidence through the countless hours of practice and games played that pushed these prodigies to the top. They were so far ahead of the curve and so much better than everyone else, and they knew it. The key was them knowing it.

That's what I missed. I knew I was good, but I always thought the next guy might be a little bit better. Now I realize you play to the level of your belief in your skill. This goes for everything in life. I could point out a top-level hooper from a mile away. They were lanky, extremely confident, slightly slue footed or pigeon toed but never square and strolled with aplomb; indifferent of the moment and never in a rush. So at ease and comfortable in their own skin, no matter how big the game. They almost seem too relaxed, bordering on lethargic. Even in the warmups before tip-off, minutes away from the championship game, everything was effortless.

I remember talking to an old teammate who was an absolute stud on the court. Rarely did he do what the coach told him to do, but he hardly ever came out of the game. He played the game on his terms, and it usually worked out for the best. I asked him, "How do you pull off so many cool moves and play so well in big games? Aren't you afraid to lose the ball or make a mistake?"

He told me something that has stuck with me to this day. He said, "It's good to be coachable, but at the same time you have to trust your instincts and skills to carry you through the game. If you only do what the coach tells you, your game becomes too robotic and you stop yourself from playing to your fullest potential. Only you know how good you really are, and you can't be afraid to mess up."

Later, I learned that this theory is applicable to life in general. Anyone who was ever great at anything had a sense of delusional belief in themselves. As a matter of fact, to be truly great in your endeavors you must have such a belief in whatever it is you are trying to accomplish that you're okay when your family, your friends, and your community disapproves. You have to have enough wherewithal and gumption to do it anyway. Just by believing in yourself you are already more than halfway there.

PRACTICE ISN'T EVERYTHING

In tenth grade I played on the sophomore basketball team for University High School. I was the starting point-guard and was a good player but didn't play to my full potential. There was a player on the freshman team by the name of Michael Williams who did play to his full potential and maybe beyond it. What baffled me was that he wasn't a better player than me by any means. His feet were slow, and his jump shot was inconsistent. He had a sloppy, uncoordinated handle, and couldn't go left if his life depended on it. Still, I watched him dominate every game. Granted, it was freshman level, but he was scoring twice, maybe three times as many points as I was in most games. I would scratch my head in disbelief almost every game as I watched him dominate. Finally, one day I had to ask him what his secret was to play so well without ever putting in extra practice to polish his skills.

What he told me blew me away. In a nonchalant voice he said, "On game days, during lunch time I make sure to play a few games against the worst players in the school to boost my confidence. By the time it's game time my confidence is so high it carries over into the real game."

"Wow, that's genius," I thought. That day Michael taught me that practice isn't everything. Yes, I admit it's the building block of confidence and mastery. Some must practice first, and develop confidence that way. But others have confidence beforehand in their ability to do something, and I would say they're likely to circumvent the process of achieving their desired goal. These are the few that the rest of us call genius.

Although I didn't make it to the NBA, what I learned from the game of basketball is invaluable. It has made me who I am today and I'm forever grateful. If I could go back and do it all over again, knowing I would never become a professional player, I surely would. What I have taken from the game has nothing to do with dribbling or shooting a ball. I have learned that if you put enough energy into something long enough you can eventually become a guru. And on the flip side, you can practice till you're blue in the face, but sooner or later you cannot second guess yourself, you just have to go for it.

CHAPTER 11

SEEING THINGS DIFFERENTLY

All human experience is one hundred percent self-created.
—Sadhguru

HAPPINESS HAS NEVER LEFT,
SO WHY ARE YOU CHASING IT?

As young children, we were boundless and free. We created so much with so little, and we were as happy as can be. Our elaborate imaginations took us on journeys to outer space where we flew around in cool rocket ships, shooting aliens with our laser guns. Or in a far, far away land with flying, fire-breathing dragons and wizards with long white beards creating magic with their wooden wands. Shortly after, we grew into pizza-face teenagers who thought we knew it all and desired nothing more than to fit in and be cool. Our malleable personalities and fragile psyches quickly drove us to clique with a group we could classify with to solidify our identities. Then as adults we shifted our focus to work, money, status, and accumulation. So much so that we revolved our entire lives around it all, and sacrificed everything to get it—including our happiness. At our core, everything we did or didn't do was to attain happiness. But in the process, happiness needed to take a back seat so everything else could get done so we could finally be happy. The paradox of sacrificing happiness to attain happiness may be the biggest oxymoron. The pursuit is vicious and has never been fulfilled. Only when we come to grips with this can we begin to experience everlasting happiness.

As far back as I can remember, I carried two lingering thoughts in the back of my mind. Is it possible to be always happy? And if so, what does the highest level of happiness feel like? For years, I thought the people with the most money were the happiest, and all the poor people were striving to get to this esoteric place. If you didn't get there, then you'd failed at life, and in the rare case that you did, then you'd "made it." You'd reached the pinnacle, heaven on earth. Something tells me I'm not the only one who felt this way. It wasn't until I was closer to the age I am now that I realized how far this is from the truth.

For most of my childhood and teenage years I lived in neighborhoods of black families who more or less earned the same amount of income. No one I knew was even close to being financially rich; and if a family did have a little more financial freedom than the rest of us, it was only a little. As I got older, I was exposed to a number of different ethnic groups and social classes. I made friends with all races and types of people. Even to this day the company I keep is a motley crew of interesting folk. Over time, I've learned and compared the norms of all different races, religions, styles of upbringings and social classes.

This exposure has given me an inside look at lifestyles I'd only seen on TV. I've had dinner with families living north of Santa Monica Blvd. in the most expensive parts of Beverly Hills. With ballroom crystal chandeliers hanging fifteen feet above white marbled floors and winding staircases. Big pearly white grand pianos conspicuously placed in the corner of their living rooms. And backyards the size of a football field with water fountains in the middle of beautiful floral gardens along with infinity pools and jacuzzi; the kind you can find on the roof of a five-star hotel or in a travel magazine. To my surprise, not only are those families human like the rest of us, but they too struggle to stay happy, and are in desperate pursuit to experience the highest level of happiness.

So why does happiness feel transient? It seems like it's always fleeting. Among other reasons, the one encompassing reason is lack of contentment. We humans have that insatiable nature about us. It has actually become our goal never to be content. No wonder happiness is always fleeting. We push it away with both hands. In addition to this primal instinct, growing up in a country like America probably doesn't help. With some sustained consciousness, we can tame it.

The word content is synonymous with happy, but it's hardly ever used interchangeably, mainly because it is commonly considered to be too subtle a form of happy. Nowadays, no one wants their happiness to be subtle. We need the world to know how happy we are all the time. We need to post it, share it, and retweet how happy we are, or else our happiness never existed. In his book Atomic Habits James Clear states, "Happiness is not about the achievement of pleasure, but about the lack of desire. It arrives when you have no urge to feel differently. Happiness is the state you enter when you no longer want to change your state." I concur. The truth is, the happiest people rarely display their happiness.

Happiness is simply our nature. There is no need to chase it because it never left. It is just that over time we have slipped back into identifying with the compulsions of the mind and body again and again and forgotten our true essence. This is why meditation is so important; it reassures you of who you are and your reason to be. Moreover, meditation puts you back in the driver's seat. It allows you to steer your life with precision. Ironically, no one has time to meditate because they are too busy chasing happiness.

NON-ATTACHMENT = FREEDOM = HAPPINESS

The gateway to this unburdened, blissful state of happiness is NON-ATTACHMENT. Most of us cannot fathom non-attachment. We comprehend it as ridding ourselves of all our nice toys and material goods, walking around barefoot like a Buddhist monk with nothing covering our body but a sheet. This isn't so. You can enjoy nice things and remain content and non-attached. In fact, you should enjoy life's pleasures. No one really knows where we go from here. The key is not to identify with anything or become too attached to it. Submerge yourself in the experience of life not the idea of it. Marvel at the beauty and uniqueness of everything and everyone you come across, and in the same breath be able to move on from it at any moment without a fuss. Temporariness is the subtle beauty of life.

Non-attachment also goes for personas we fall into and then identify with—our occupation, ourselves as parents, siblings, friends, and lovers. I see this all the time. We hold ourselves and others to an obligatory role we identify with based on societal norms. If you first understand that most things about our society aren't normal, then you are well on your way to liberation and happiness. Parents will say, "This is MY son or daughter, So-and-so." Or a husband will say, "This is MY wife, so-and-so." This is fine for introduction purposes or letting someone know the relation between you and this person. Again, the problem lies in the attachment of the identity. We really start to believe this person is OUR son or OUR wife. Like a possession. We buy into these roles and convince ourselves this is who we are. Instead, you should see the title as a transitory verb and not a solidified noun. Then your actions with that person are more important rather than the title you hold. Identification with the title indubitably breeds a sense of entitlement. If each person can set their perspective in this way their intentions will inevitably follow. Right away that'll create a disconnection from the identity, eliminating rigidity and opening up space for the relationship to be and flow organically. Each person will feel a sense of freedom, paradoxically pulling them closer together.

Keep in mind that freedom is less about physical space and more about mental and spiritual elbowroom. Every person has a whole world inside of them that needs sorting day by day, minute by minute, second by second. Try not to be selfish and push your world on top of theirs. For anyone this is a difficult feat. Sort yours out yourself, for this is the reason you exist. This shift in understanding alone could save millions of relationships of all textures. So again, become present and submerge yourself in the experience of the relationship and let go of the idea of it. Every relationship is unique with its own language. If you can do this, the voice of the relationship will tell you what it requires to be healthy.

Keep in mind that people are not possessions, and they don't owe you anything. Better yet, keep in mind that you don't own anything. That suit you call a body that you are glued to is on lease. At some point you must give it back to the rightful owner. So don't get too comfortable in that thing. Before you know it, the return date will come. Just enjoy the damn thing while you can. Treat it like a car rental. You can either go for the speed racing Lamborghini or the pragmatic, ecofriendly Kia, or anything in between. The choice is yours.

PLEASURE
HAPPINESS
CONTENTMENT

Pleasure, happiness, and contentment are like the building blocks of a pyramid. Pleasure is the pinnacle, contentment is the foundation, and happiness is the core. Naturally, we want to experience life at the pinnacle. So, the aim is always up. This is especially the case when we are young and full of energy. We literally wish to fly. As we get older, we generally become wiser as we settle into the ebb and flow of life. We maintain our perspective and see life for what it is. We've smartened up and no longer need to exert ourselves as we once did. We understand that if we want to see the top all we need to do is look up.

To be in a pleasurable mood is wonderful. The thing is, when you're this high up the fall is much further, potentially leaving you shattered at the bottom. To be this high up you will first need to establish a clear perspective to help maintain your balance. This perspective can only be constructed on the ground level, like everything else. Once the foundation is built you can go upward and you never have to come down.

OUT OF BODY, OUT OF MIND, OUT OF SIGHT

One overcast Saturday morning, I was taking a walk with one of my friends who's about eight years older than me. She told me something that was very spiritual, but I don't think she realized it at the time. I was in my late twenties at the time, and I asked her what my thirties would be like. She told me, "The older you get, the less you'll care about what others think of you." That simple statement blew me away, and in that moment, I knew she was right. Not only was she right, but later I realized that this is the same idea most spiritual gurus talk about when they speak of freeing yourself from the ego and living within the spirit.

As a youngster I had plenty of friends I truly enjoyed spending time with. In the same breath, my extensive imagination allowed me to play alone for hours on end. Sometimes a whole day would go by without me ever engaging with anyone else. I'd look up, see the sun was setting, and know my grandmother was in the kitchen preparing dinner. An insatiable craving to explore my inner layers has always been my calling—over anything else.

As a kid I used to do this weird thing that I've never told anyone about until now. Sometimes, after I would wash my hands in the bathroom, I would lean my forearms on the mouth of the sink and stare directly into the mirror, focusing right into the pupils of my eyes. After a minute or so, my surroundings deaden, I could feel a subtle disconnection from the body; it felt like I was two people. The body of me standing there and the observer of the body of me standing there. Even then I knew I was the observer manifested into this representation of me. I would murmur, "Okay, so this is you, De'Sean. This is who everyone sees. This is the body G-d gave you. Pretty cool. Thanks, G-d!" It was like I had information that no one else had. I saw it as my body being a huge human-looking robotic machine and I was hiding inside viewing the world through the eyes; operating the machine with pulleys, buttons and levers. Like that little alien on the first Men in Black movie. After my imagination took me there, I would crack a smirk and walk out all giddy and jolly. I realize now, that in a way, this was a form of meditation. Or at least me identifying that there is more to me than just the physical.

My entire life I've lived with my head in the clouds. Always wondering what else is out there. Do aliens exist? Where do we go after we die? Is G-d's pronoun he, she or it? I've been curious about everything and questioned everything. I'm still this way. Supposed answers only created more questions for me. Even now, I can hardly ever come to a conclusion with anything because I accept other possibilities to be true—including personal experiences. I understand that from the moment I was born I have been conditioned to experience life in a certain way. And this experience is only a part of my truth but not necessarily the whole truth. This way of thinking creates endless possibilities (which I love) but also leaves me with an overwhelming amount of unanswered questions (which can be nettlesome). Placing my feet on fragile ground has always been a bit scary, but also exhilarating. Overall, I prefer it to be this way. It has left me silent in debates and misunderstood in arguments. I've come to terms with that too. I've learned that no one really knows what they are talking about, but it sure sounds like they do. Now I just nod and smile.

In addition to getting older and not giving a hoot what others think about me, I gradually started meditating. The very first time I tried it I knew there was something to it. I couldn't fully explain it (I still can't, though I'm better at it now), but I was certain there was something to it. Intuitively, I knew meditation was a powerful tool that could enhance the quality of life. But because of its simplicity and nothingness it was difficult to wrap my logical mind around it. Like most of us, I refused to make it a priority. It was too easy to do and even easier not to do. In my first experience there was a noticeable detachment from all life's issues. But this sense of serenity faded quickly. Honking horns, screaming sirens, and a ringing phone that needed to be answered right away sucked me back into the loud and messy scramble of life. I was shaken like a pair of dice on a hot Vegas craps table. Shortly after that, my mind was inundated with questions. So I surfed the web for answers. How long should I meditate? What should I be feeling? What should I be thinking? How do I prevent my lower back from getting tired? After a few hours surfing the web my eyes were crossed and I could hear a pulse in my head. All that time spent and now it seemed like I had more questions than before. Overall, the consensus was that there is no right or wrong way to meditate. There are many different forms of meditation, and each individual will practice what is suitable for him or her. Start with a small amount of time, focus on the breath, and do it daily, meditation will take care of the rest.

The anticipation of my child's arrival sparked something in me that only the love of my child could spark. A rebirth. After the breakup I literally did some self-reflecting. One night, after brushing my teeth, I stared at myself in my bathroom mirror. Kind of how I used to do when I was a kid, only this time I wasn't trying to do that meditation trick. I just stared. Some time went by and I continued to stare. After a while, my eyes began to water and out of nowhere, I started to cry. I didn't bawl. I just had a blank stare and tears began to roll down my cheeks to the floor—one by one. Without a blink, tears continued to stream. At first, I didn't know why I was crying. I didn't even think about it. I just cried. A minute or so passed, and then I noticed something different about me. I became unrecognizable to myself. Flashes of when I was a young boy appeared in my mind. My body grew heavy in disappointment. I knew I hadn't done my best and I wondered why. "Where did I go?" I wondered. "Where did the real me go? What happened to me?"

My child's impending arrival reminded me of promises I had made to myself when I was a kid that I had never lived up to. I remember saying to myself, "When I grow up and have kids, I'm going to be the best dad!" I had a vision of how my life was going to be. I remember the innocence in my voice and the optimism in my heart. I had let that innocent part of me down. I could not let my child down.

After moving into my own space, I began immediately to reprogram myself. A high level of disconnection from the world was necessary in order for me to reconnect with the source. I was in pursuit of my essence. So every morning at 5:00 a.m. I sat with my eyes closed and listened to my breath for thirty-five to forty-five minutes. I did this for roughly four hundred and fifty days and counting, without fail. At the start, I wasn't sure what the act of this practice could offer but I knew without a doubt if I could maintain this habit, I could maintain any. This habit turned ritual freed me from me. I became so peaceful within, nothing or no one could disturb it. Every day was fluid and effortless. I no longer struggled, or in the few times that I did, I simply altered my perspective and the situation became docile.

More than anything, meditation is a constant reminder of how to keep perspective. Over time and with continual practice, my perspective has drastically sharpened. This strengthen ability was especially important as I continued to reinforce new habits and destroy old ones. Eventually, my days were consumed with meditation, reading, writing, physical exercise, a vegetarian diet, and work. At first glance, my schedule not only looked boring but it would be difficult to maintain. Initially, I thought the same thing. But as I said earlier, "I simply changed my perspective and the situation became docile." My seemingly dull and arduous day turned into an exciting day filled with opportunities to grow, learn, play, imagine, create, feast on quality foods, and see the world from the highest viewpoint imaginable. A brother of mine once told me years ago, "Once you head down this journey of awareness, it pulls you in and you never go back."

CHAPTER 12

WUBAS

Love is your quality.
Love is not what you do.
Love is what you are.
—Sadhguru

On January 26, 2020, my favorite basketball player of all time, Kobe Bryant, "The Black Mamba," died, along with his thirteen-year-old daughter Gigi, in a helicopter crash. Kobe was my role model in every way imaginable. On that same day my daughter celebrated her first birthday in Sydney, Australia, without me. As I sat on my bed in disbelief and mused over the magnitude of the day, I recognized the stillness of my energy. In my mind I kept thinking, "Why am I not a wreck? My favorite player of all time just died and I'm missing my daughter's first birthday." I couldn't make it make sense logically, but I knew something in me had changed. After I sat and mused on each event for a few minutes I then proceeded on with my day.

On January 26, 2019, in Sydney, Australia, Aaliyah Sarai Compton-Stacy was born. Though we were apart, Britt and I continued to struggle to keep the peace between us during her second and third trimester. That struggle led to many breaks in our communication, at what was supposed to be one of the most special times of our lives. We couldn't go for more than a few days without an explosive argument. Britt would yell or cry, which triggered me to withdraw. After the smoke settled, all I could think of was the health of the baby. I worried about Aaliyah during most of Britt's pregnancy. I knew something had to be done for the sake of our unborn child. I began to realize that the only solution for peace was for us not to communicate. This killed me but I knew it was the only way.

On April 12, 2019, at 5:38 p.m. I was in Beverly Hills in the middle of a training session, timing a client on her plank. A WhatsApp notification slid down from the top of my screen, showing, "Photo message from Brittany Compton." My heart pounded as right away I knew what it was about. I slid down the picture and cupped my hand over my mouth. Looking like a baby angel Aaliyah laid there swathed in a white cloth up to her chest. She was perfect in every sense. After the session I sat in the car and marveled at the photo of our beautiful daughter. My cheeks ached from smiling too much, but I couldn't help myself. I was so proud and overwhelmed with joy. Oddly enough, I slowly became conflicted and filled with anger. I kept thinking, "Why is this the first time I'm seeing Aaliyah? It has been almost three months since she was born!" Then I recalled that four days before Aaliyah's birth I had received a long ornery text from Britt, and at the end of it she had asked me to stay out of her life and Aaliyah's life. I knew this text was sent out of anger and frustration, and at that moment I knew I was going to miss the birth of my first born. This was a tough pill to swallow, but I never thought it would be almost three months after her birth before we spoke again. The rhythm of breaks in our relationship had been happening since the conception of Aaliyah. Numerous times we vowed, for our daughter's sake, not to let ourselves split apart. Sadly, we were unsuccessful at bringing the idea to life.

The night was falling while I sat in the car in disbelief, deepening the pain of missing Aaliyah's birth. I began to think about my father, absent for most of my childhood, coming back into my life in my early twenties. I recalled a profound conversation I had with him some years back. We were at his brother's family get together standing on the front lawn chatting about life. He had been drinking a bit, so the truth was flowing. He said to me with the utmost sincerity, "Seany Mack! I'm sorry I had to go when you were a kid. But it was for the best. I was not a good person back then. I was reckless and wild." I nodded my head in understanding. His eyes began to well up with tears and his voice started to shake as he said to me, "I'm so proud of your mother and how she raised you and your brother. You are both such good young men. I'm so proud of the person you are and the kindness you hold in your heart. If I would've stuck around, you probably wouldn't be this way." I said I knew that, and then we hugged. This memory abated the pain and gave me perspective on my current situation.

Although my attitude had improved, I still needed a couple of days to iron out my emotions before I could respond to Britt with poise. She and I played phone tag for a couple of days, trying to line up a conversation. Finally, after a few days we were able to sync our schedules and speak over the phone. There were so many difficult things we needed to address. I wanted to hop right to the nitty gritty, but since we hadn't spoken in a while there was a befitting subtleness early on. Aaliyah's frequent soft cries in the background urged me to ask Britt to FaceTime throughout the conversation. Just hearing Aaliyah's voice made me smile. This longing to be with her was killing me. After some small talk followed by the blame game, we finally FaceTimed for about thirty minutes. I was stunned by Aaliyah's beauty and head size. Her head was wide and round, full of dark and curly hair that laid on the outer edges of her face like silk. There was a certain glow about her I had never seen before. It was like a light was emitting through her honey complexion. Her deep dark brown almond-shaped eyes stared back at me with awareness and precision.

I have no recollection of what was said between Britt and me at this moment. I just remember resting my chin in my hand, amazed at our daughter. Thirty minutes felt like five, and before I knew it we were hanging up. For a reason I'm still unsure of but we didn't speak again until May on Mother's Day, via text. I'd sent a few texts between April 23 and May 11, but I got no response. I must have said or done something she was not happy with. Or maybe she was tied up and overwhelmed with being a new mother. It wasn't long before we had another argument about our past that triggered another break. On August 21 I was able to see Aaliyah through FaceTime again, and Britt and I worked out a day for me to visit them in Sydney Australia.

GOO GOO GAA GAA

On October 2, 2019 I flew across the sea to Sydney, Australia, and met my daughter in person for the first time. That was the happiest day of my life. From the moment we locked eyes, my life changed forever.

After about a thirty-minute wait in the smoke-filled terminal, my phone rang, and "Brittany Compton" showed on the screen. My heart started to beat like a drum. I got so excited and nervous at the same time. I had imagined this moment over and over a hundred times.

"Where is your terminal?" Britt asked.

"I'm at terminal 1 next to this parking lot full of taxis. Where are you?" I responded.

"Underneath these big brown umbrellas where a bunch of people are sitting."

"Ugh, I don't see you guys. Do you know where I am? Do you know how to get to me? I'm at terminal 1," I repeated impatiently. "I'm wearing a gray sweater and a camouflage backpack. I'm waving my hand; do you see me?!"

"Turn around. I think I see you," she said. I turned around and saw her walking towards me pushing a dark navy stroller. I began to walk towards them. I smiled so hard it hurt. I couldn't contain myself. As I got closer, everything and everyone else at the terminal faded away. I put down my duffle bag along with my luggage and gave Britt a big hug. She had this awkward, shy smile that she always got when we hadn't seen each other in a while.

Then I turned around and leaned down into the stroller as she pulled back the canopy. My heart stopped, awestruck that anyone could be so beautiful. We locked eyes for a moment, then Aaliyah quickly shifted her gaze to Britt for approval, unfamiliar with who I was.

"Take her out, take her out right now," I repeated. I fumbled with the belt wrapped around Aaliyah's shoulders, her soft hand gently laid on top of mine as her mother easily unlocked her out of the safety strap. Britt reached in and grabbed underneath Aaliyah's chubby arms and handed her to me. I hugged her so tightly and kissed her rosy cheeks a hundred times. Before I knew it, Aaliyah started to cry and began to look for her mother. Britt wiped her own tears as I handed Aaliyah back to her. I continued to maul her fat cheeks and her neck that smelled of milk.

The clement weather and metropolitan district of Sydney reminded me of Los Angeles. Britt, Aaliyah, and I had breakfast almost every morning at what came to be my favorite breakfast spot in Sydney. I'm ashamed I can't recall the name, but I sure do remember the experience. I got the same thing every time: organic steel cut oatmeal sprinkled with almond flakes, with a handful of dates buried throughout, drizzled in honey and a few splashes of raw almond milk and a cup of coffee.

For those few days I felt like we were a normal family. I got my first chance to be a dad and I loved it! In the middle of the night loud wails startled me out of deep sleep. In the pitch-dark Britt or I would get up and coddle Aaliyah back to sleep. Only to be awakened in another hour to do it all over again. Each day I watched Britt take on the tedious task of being a parent. This was her first child, and Aaliyah was only ten months young, but Britt already seemed like a pro. She got herself and Aaliyah dressed and prepared the diaper bag each time we left the hotel. She made it seem easy, though I didn't think it was. I never heard her complain—except for one crucial time.

By the fifth day of my visit things started to feel routine—but in a good way. As a unit we had caught a rhythm. Britt pushed the stroller, as I carried Aaliyah and then struggled to strap her in the car seat when it was time for us to leave. But one day we both dropped the ball. We were all in my hotel room about to head back out to the hotel's gym for a quick workout. Britt had just tended to Aaliyah and laid her in the center of the bed with her toy. I was sitting at the foot of the bed talking to Britt. She walked past me pulling my eyes along with her. While we were still talking, she knelt on the floor to search inside her bag for a hair tie. She didn't fully kneel, but before she could completely stand, we hear a loud thud.

As soon as I heard it, I knew what had happened. An indescribable feeling came over me. We both rushed over to the side of the bed to find our daughter lying on her back with her fist clinched and her face as red as a cherry. Aaliyah screamed at the top of her lungs as Brittany quickly swooped her from the floor. Britt cradled and soothed her, but Aaliyah was too shaken up to stop crying for another ten minutes. As she began to quiet down, I began feel that everything was going to be okay. Still, I was sick about what had just happened.

Britt was very shaken and wanted to go to a doctor immediately. We packed our stuff and rushed to the nearest emergency room. After the doctor examined Aaliyah, she mentioned a few things to look out for within the next twenty-four to forty-eight hours, saying our child was just fine. We were so relieved and grateful.

Although we were exhausted, we thought it would be a good idea to get a workout in to relieve some stress and take our minds off what just happened. Later, we got ready and all went to dinner.

This was my fifth night in Sydney, Australia. Britt was driving us to dinner, but she was having a hard time understanding the directions on her phone. Aaliyah and I were fast asleep with our heads fallen back and mouths wide open like two Venus flytraps. At this point, those sleepless nights had really worn on me. I realized I had been sleepy my whole stay there. On this night you couldn't have paid me to keep my eyelids peeled. Britt grew frustrated from making so many wrong turns and got on the phone with her sister Lauren to see if she could be of any help. I guess the restaurant was in an area they were both unfamiliar with since her sister wasn't really able to help her either. "Sean!" she yelled. It startled me out of my slumber.

"Yeah," I responded groggily.

"Do you know how to get there?" she asked.

"Britt, this is my first time in your country. How would I know how to get somewhere I've never been?"

"I don't know, but I'm lost and all you do is lie there and fall asleep leaving me to figure everything out. Why do I have to do everything? I have to get Aaliyah ready, get myself dressed, figure out what restaurant we're going to, drive, and figure out how to get to the restaurant. You don't do anything! You just sit there and play with Aaliyah and fall asleep."

"Britt, if we were in my country, I would have to do what you're doing. And you can't include getting yourself and Aaliyah ready. That's something you would do even if I wasn't here. Don't I take care of everything when you're in L.A? I don't ask you for directions in my own city. That doesn't make any sense. Anyway, let me see your phone so I can figure out how to get to the restaurant in your city." She handed me the phone and took a deep sigh. "Britt! You gotta hit the 'GO' button so it can start the route. If you don't, then the map will keep swiveling, disorienting you every time you make a turn," I said, holding my forehead in disbelief. "Jesus, Britt!"

"Oh, okay. I was wondering why the map kept turning around like that," she responded in an airhead kind of way. We had a laugh as she continued to drive. A few minutes later she apologized for snapping at me. "It just that everything seems so hard and I'm just tired. I just want things to go smoothly while you're here," Britt said after apologizing. I told her I understood. We pulled up in the parking lot and everything seemed to be okay.

While we were waiting to be seated, I could sense there was still something unsettled in Britt. I couldn't put my finger on what it could be, since we had just had a lighthearted laugh about her not understanding how to use Google Map. I thought everything had worked itself out. In moments like this I could always sense when things were about to go bad. The quiet before the storm was worse than the storm. The knowing and anticipation killed me. It always felt like I was chained to the ground, watching this huge tornado slowly head towards me. No matter what I did or how hard I struggled, there was no way of escaping. For me, this was the worst feeling. These moments conjured memories from my childhood when I would hear my parents arguing down the hall. In the moment of those heated arguments I made a promise to myself to never to put my kid through that. I absolutely hated how it made me feel, and I never wanted my child to experience that feeling. These moments with Britt triggered that familiar "sick to my stomach" feeling I used to get when I watched or heard my parents argue.

After a while the waiter finally came over and walked us to our table. "It's the fifth day, our usual breaking point," flashed in my head. I said a short silent prayer, asking to get us through the night in one piece. Foreboding had struck me here and there throughout the day. The tension was thick, you could cut it with a knife. Britt had that familiar glare in her eyes she gives me whenever something is bothering her. At first, I ignored it and stared out the window pretending to be interested in the seagulls fighting over scraps near the harbor. Then I casually mentioned how beautifully the light from the moon glistened on the ripples of the water. I played a little goo goo gaa gaa with Aaliyah to delay the inevitable. Even the bizarre, desperate thought of us not talking through the whole dinner briefly entered my mind.

Eventually, Britt got fed up and said, "Hello! Are you going to speak to me!?" I sat there dumbfounded. I didn't know what to say. I knew anything I said would be risky. I was terrified, so I said, "What's up?" as if I was unaware of the awkward silence that had taken place for the past twenty minutes. Answering with that stupid response made everything worse. We went back and forth over dinner for a bit. Britt's voice gradually rose in frustration. Not only did this make me uncomfortable, but I didn't want to argue in front of our daughter or in the restaurant. We couldn't be the family that yelled and argued in public. I simply refused to do it. So I went silent, boxed up my food, and walked towards the exit. I realized there was no way to salvage the night and no way to resolve our discussion.

She yelled my name a few times as I ignored her and continued walking. I knew I had nowhere to go, but I just couldn't argue or be yelled at in public. As I was walking all I could think of was, "It's late and I'm really far from my hotel." My wheels were turning a mile a minute with thoughts of possible ways to get back to the hotel without riding with Britt and Aaliyah. I quickly checked my phone battery: 11 percent. "I just have to ride this one out," I concluded. The whole day had been a disaster, and the drive back to the hotel wasn't any better.

After four hours of Britt giving me the third degree, I thought she was finally done. I was sitting on the bed with my back against the headrest rocking Aaliyah to sleep. Britt walked around to our side of the bed and started to speak and behave in a way that showed she was fired up all over again, and I feared for Aaliyah's comfort. I felt that Britt wasn't going to stop whether I stayed quiet or not. I thought to myself, "Enough is enough!" I slowly laid Aaliyah in the middle of the bed, stood up from a lounging position, and roared, "WHAT THE FUCK IS WRONG WITH YOU!!!" Inches from Britt's face. Her body cringed as she stood there aghast as if she saw a ghost.

"Oh my god! Oh my god! I'm calling the police! I can't believe you just did that. Oh my god, I'm shaking. Where's my phone?" I took a quick glance at Aaliyah and calmly watched Britt stagger around the room in search of her cell phone. Her hands trembled as she scrolled through her contacts. She called her mom but got no answer. Then she dialed 000.

"What are you doing, Britt?"

"I'm calling the police, this isn't safe. I can't believe you did that in front of our daughter."

"Oh, now it isn't safe? You've been having a go at me the whole night, and I stayed quiet and practically begged you to stop and you didn't! But now it isn't safe!? Get the hell outta here with that! I don't know why you're calling the police—nothing happened. You need to hang up and leave, Britt." I took a deep sigh. I couldn't believe she actually went through with the call.

"Look at how sacred Aaliyah is!" she said as she waited for the police to answer.

"Britt, she's just lying there." The operator answered. Britt stammered trying to explain what happened. Then it hit me, "She's really calling the police on me." I was shocked. I couldn't believe it. "This has never happened before," I thought in utter disbelief. I realized that the cops were coming even if she hung up the phone in that moment. So I quickly pulled out my phone and started recording the whole thing. After she spent fifteen minutes on the phone with the operator, I helped Britt carry her and Aaliyah's stuff downstairs to her car.

As I walked out of the elevator back to my hotel room, I heard pounding on a door down the hall. "Hi, officer, that's my room. How can I help you?"

"Are you De'Sean Stacy?"

"Yes I am. Please let's go into the room, it's late and I don't want to talk in the hall." There were two officers. One was a short, stocky Asian man with broad shoulders named Martin, and the other was a tall Caucasian fella about 6'2" with dirty blonde hair. His name was Chris, and he wasn't fat, but he didn't look like he missed many meals. Chris and I did most of the talking, while Martin chimed in here and there. Martin had a reserve about him, and for the most part he stood next to us and jotted down notes. Meanwhile, I rocked back and forth in the desk chair and answered all their questions, untroubled and confident it was all going to be over soon. After about fifteen minutes of questioning, there was a quiet knock at the door. Martin walked over to open it, but he never asked who it was, he just opened it. A short, slightly built guy who was also Caucasian walked in. I didn't see the name on his badge; he spoke to officer Martin for a quick second and then they both left the room. Apparently, the other officer who had just walked in had caught Britt in the underground parking structure before she left. The three officers went back and forth from the room to the parking structure for about forty-five minutes as we both gave our versions of what happened.

Chris was the only officer who told me he believed my story. Simply because I had most of the altercation recorded on my phone. Then he turned around and told me, "But my partner wants to look into it for further investigation. So we're gonna have to arrest you and take you down to the station for further questioning."

All I heard was "ARREST YOU."

"ARREST ME?!" I responded. "FOR WHAT!? THIS IS MY ROOM AND SHE WAS LEAVING. WHY AM I GETTING ARRESTED?!

WHAT IS THE CHARGE?!"

"Intimidation," he responded.

"INTIMIDATION!?" I repeated. I knew there was no sense in arguing so I quickly grabbed my crew neck sweatshirt from the arm of the desk chair and tossed it over my head. They escorted me out of my hotel room and into the back of a cold police truck at 2 a.m. in Chatswood, Australia. I walked out wearing pajama shorts and a crew neck sweatshirt with a bad cop joke on the front of it.

A BEAUTIFULLY ADVERSE SITUATION

On the lengthy flight back from Australia I had plenty of time to think. The moments I had shared with my daughter I reflected on the most. Her big round face and rosy cheeks were all I could think of. The scent of sour milk tucked underneath her short neck that I loved to inhale while I poured on the kisses. Or even in the middle of the night when she woke up crying and I would hold her to my chest while I paced the hotel room rocking her back to sleep. In those indelible moments I felt like a dad. My daughter reminded me of what unconditional love truly is.

Blended with the memories I shared with my beautiful daughter was the deep-rooted memory of the night I spent in jail. The night replayed in my mind over and over on the flight back home. They put me into this tiny holding cell the size of a phone booth. The policeman left the bulletproof glass door that was covered in graffiti and lined with metal bars slightly open in case I needed to use the restroom. He also gave me a thin and dusty blanket in case I got cold. These were nice gestures, but I was still in jail. Time crawled like a two-legged turtle while I sat, slumped on the short, cold metal bench that protruded from the etiolated walls blotched with chipped paint. After a while my eyelids were closed for business, I could no longer sit up. My head would nod every few seconds, and my body would follow right behind it. So I folded the dusty blanket into a pillow then curled my stiff, achy body into a ball and tried for some sleep.

The short bench was smooth and had a slight downward tilt. Any movement sent me sliding off onto the floor. After hitting the floor a couple of times, I stood up and leaned against the wall. I listened to my stomach growl like a vicious watch dog as my exhausted body melted into the walls of the holding cell. The realization that I was confined to jail weighed on me heavily. I knew this wasn't a place I belonged. Although I knew I was innocent, thoughts of horrible outcomes began to run across my mind. "There are plenty of people in jail or prison who are innocent. How will I afford a lawyer?" I worried.

"Hey, would you like anything to eat? We have some crappy TV dinners if you like," the policeman said, interrupting my thoughts.

"That's okay, but thanks," I replied, thinking snobbishly that I shouldn't subject myself to the likes of that stuff.

Even back in L.A., I couldn't shake thoughts of how my trip to Australia ended. After the police let me out of the holding cell at 10 a.m., I spent the rest of my morning catching a bunch of different buses to the courtroom for a hearing. After being forced to plead guilty because I couldn't afford to stay in Australia for another month or so for my next official hearing, I caught the train back to the police station to retrieve my belongings. Then I walked for forty-five minutes in the rain back to my hotel room.

Unexpectedly, Britt called me at the hotel that night. We spoke for a few hours about the whole thing. She apologized, and the next morning she picked me up from the hotel and took me to the airport. There was no pause in our communication. We spoke as if the night I'd spent in jail had never happened. It was late December before she mentioned that horrid night. "I was shocked that you were willing to speak to me at all, and that you forgave me so quickly," she divulged. "I would never have forgiven you so quickly."

"I forgave you for me, Britt. The weight of hate and resentment is much too heavy for me to bear." Even hunched over in the cell in Chatswood I forgave her for calling the cops on me. Forgiveness changed my whole demeanor right there in jail. Even though my stomach was growling, and I could barely hold my head up to keep from nodding off and my mind went to a dark place here and there, my spirit was at peace.

FORGIVENESS

Forgiveness is a spiritual detox for the forgiver and restores the perspective of the forgiven. Forgiveness restores the natural order of things. No one can carry the burden of a grudge for any real length of time without it festering into malignancy. The bitterness will contaminate every element of the self. When we can find it within ourselves to forgive, we free ourselves of animosity and cleanse that space of pain, initiating a process of liberation and healing. But most people wait too long to forgive. They hold on to the pain as a reminder to one day get even, permitting the hurt to deepen and cause more damage. They cannot fathom moving on and letting go so quickly. For some, that bottled pain eventually kills them. "I have to get even! How can I make them feel what I felt so they won't ever mistreat me or anyone else like this again? I must teach them a lesson!" These are the common thoughts that linger in the mind and the heart of the hurt. As a result, the initial affliction swells. Getting even turns you into the person you despise. It actually puts you below the one who has hurt you, because you become knowingly wicked. This perpetuates a toxic, cancerous cycle that cannot be broken by revenge.

You must release that hurt. It's not for you to carry, let alone keep. Vindictiveness is poisonous and draining only to the person carrying it. I believe deep down on some level this thought process has nothing to do with getting even. Deeper than that, it's about teaching compassion. But you can't teach compassion with revenge on the mind. You can't teach it by making the assailant feel what you felt. Forgiveness is the way to teach compassion. When you can find it within yourself to forgive someone, you are teaching them compassion and freeing yourself all at once.

This virtuous act can stifle the cycle of recrimination. Only then can you grow as a person. You must rise above getting even and position yourself in virtue. Because when someone handles you roughly, it's never because of you. As I said before, everyone has a whole world inside of them they're sorting out day by day, minute by minute, second by second. So never take things personally, because it never is because of you or what you did. Even if they say it is, it's not. It can't be. It's not within our nature to intentionally inflict pain on one another. We've just been through some things and inside we're still working them out. We must be patient with our fellow brothers and sisters and understand that we're all growing, just at different paces. Show compassion and be love always.

THANK YOU

I thank you, Brittany Compton, the mother of my first-born child. If it wasn't for you, this book would not have been written. The struggles of our relationship help mold me into a better person. I also thank you for all the beautiful moments we've shared. Without them our little Wubas (Aaliyah), could not exist. Thank you for bringing me the most incredible gift anyone can receive, a child.

Ron and Lilach West, I thank you for always looking out for me, and for letting Britt and me live in your guest house rent free. You have always opened your home to me. More importantly, thank you for displacing us when you did. At the time I saw it to be untimely and unfortunate. In retrospect it was perfect. It was extremely uncomfortable, but you helped turn an oversize boy into a man. We are forever family.

My favorite cousin, Chace Marigny and my best friend, George Bochorishvilli, thank you for letting us crash at your place for a few nights while I figured out our next move. And for listening to me vent when I was really going through it.

Mom, thank you for always being there for me no matter how much of an inconvenience it was to you. I've tried not to bother you too much, but I've seen you bend over backwards for other people many times throughout your life, so I know it's the nature of who you are. You are the embodiment of an angel. I couldn't ask for a better mom. Also thank you for always believing in my dreams and encouraging me to press on. You've always been my number one supporter.

Dad, thank you for coming back into my life at the perfect time. Let's continue to build.

My dearest Nana, you've loved me like no other. Since I was a young boy you've made me feel like a prince. My heart is with you.

Uncle Keith and Auntie Monique Stacy, you are my second parents and you treat me like your first son. Your love, support, and guidance are beyond appreciated. When I get on, I'm taking you guys on a vacation.

Angelica Bibbins, thank you for always helping me to believe in myself. Sometimes I think you believe in me more than I do. Those talks we had in Simply's parking lot helped me more than you know.

To all my closest friends and other family members I didn't name, I thank you all too. You all help and encourage me to keep striving.

To Diana Lipnick-Feld, my Jewish mom, thank you for drawing the cover of the book. It's perfect in every way. You nailed it with Aaliyah's chubby knees. And the talks we have about life are perfect too.

To my editor, client, friend, Daniel Kiefer. Thank you for editing my first book and for all the support over the years. Your willingness to help me is truly appreciated. To Michael Wolfe, my publishing consultant. We went back and forth on details of the book many times. Your patience and understanding were perfect. You helped guide me while giving me ample elbow room to be me. For me, that was most important. DeNiro Elliot, I appreciate you cousin, you really helped bring to life the aesthetics of everything, not to mention your assistance in finalizing certain decisions I ping-ponged with you. And To Michael Quanci, my book designer. Thank you for tying all the pieces together.

My grandma, Annie V. Armstrong, who transitioned right before I was able to finish this book, thank you, for life. Thank you for your spiritual guidance. Thank you for keeping me close to G-d. Thank you for teaching me the importance of fasting. Thank you for giving me fruit when I asked for candy. Thank you for making me eat salads with every dinner. Thank you for putting jigsaw puzzles together with me. Thank you for staying up late nights to finish typing my unfinished book reports that I struggled with. Thanks for helping me study for the spelling bee contest in fourth grade. We won that second-place trophy together! Thank you for taking me to Kenneth Hahn Park for hikes, fun volleyball games, walks on the cobblestones in the shallow river, and exciting tumbles down the tall grass hills. Your spirit will forever live through me. I miss you dearly.

EXCERPT FROM MY FORTHCOMING BOOK
TO WUBAS

12/21/19
Home, 10:22 p.m.

Dear Wubas,

You came to visit your Dad before Christmas and your birthday which falls in the new year. Unfortunately, your last day here didn't end well. Your daddy and mommy got into an argument and Daddy called the police and Grandma so you and Mommy could make it back to Australia safely. Your daddy and mommy love each other but not always do we understand each other. You got a chance to meet your grandma, Uncle Eddie and your dying great-grandma, Annie V. You took a liking to your Uncle Eddie. Your mom and I think you already share some of his ways. Wubs, I have such a good time with you. I think I kissed you a million times while you were here. I couldn't help myself. I just wanna kiss and hug and squeeze you to pieces. I think I may miss you for your first birthday. Daddy and Mommy need to work some things out before Daddy can come see you again. Goodbye for now and be well my dear. I love you...

CPSIA information can be obtained
at www.ICGtesting.com
Printed in the USA
JSHW021540140821
17822JS00001BA/5